Books of Merit

Home Free

The Myth of the Empty Nest

Marni Jackson

THOMAS ALLEN PUBLISHERS
TORONTO

Library and Archives Canada Cataloguing in Publication

Jackson, Marni
    Home free : the myth of the empty nest / Marni Jackson.

ISBN 978-0-88762-616-6

1. Parent and adult child.   2. Jackson, Marni.   I. Title.

HQ755.86.J32 2010   306.874   C2010-903801-0

Editor: Patrick Crean
Cover design: Sputnik Design Partners Inc.
Cover image: Shutterstock

Published by Thomas Allen Publishers,
a division of Thomas Allen & Son Limited,
145 Front Street East, Suite 209,
Toronto, Ontario M5A 1E3 Canada

www.thomas-allen.com

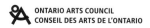

ONTARIO ARTS COUNCIL
CONSEIL DES ARTS DE L'ONTARIO

Canada Council
for the Arts

The publisher gratefully acknowledges the support of
The Ontario Arts Council for its publishing program.

We acknowledge the support of the Canada Council for the Arts, which
last year invested $20.1 million in writing and publishing throughout Canada.

We acknowledge the Government of Ontario through the
Ontario Media Development Corporation's Ontario Book Initiative.

We acknowledge the financial support of the Government of Canada
through the Canada Book Fund (CBF) for our publishing activities.

1 2 3 4 5   14 13 12 11 10

Printed and bound in Canada

for Olive and Lola

You can't be twenty on Sugar Mountain
Though you're thinking that
You're leavin' there too soon.

— Neil Young

Contents

Home Free

Treacheries

An Introduction

It's a humid spring day, and my 26-year-old son has just biked across town, from the apartment he shares with some friends, to tackle a strange chore. He's sitting at the table in our kitchen, reading the last few chapters of this book, which tells the story of our family from the time he left home at 18 to go to college in Montreal to last year, when he moved back to Toronto. I am nervous; I have no idea whether my version of things will square with his.

I don't expect him to be enthralled. It's bad enough getting a string of emails from your mother about job prospects without having to read an entire book written by your mother, about being a mother.

So I have to distract myself while he reads, pen in hand. I go upstairs and decide to throw out all our expired prescription drugs. That takes five minutes. I check my email and sign a few online petitions. I look out my office window and see Casey down below. He's moved out to the table on the patio. He's turning the pages, making a note now and then. From this angle I can't tell if he looks annoyed or just neutral. The suspense is driving me crazy.

We've been through this process before, with him reading the stories I've written about our family, getting backstage glimpses of me as mother. I have writerly tricks, but if I am not telling the truth he will be the first to detect this. At the same time, I need to stand up for how I see things, too. How it felt for me when he left home, went off to school, dropped out, roamed around Mexico, came back . . . how the three of us have negotiated the ongoing shifting of our roles.

His response to this project has been patient, and his advice has been useful. "Just be true to your own experience of things," he said, "and don't confuse that with who I am."

The other editorial insight he gave me was this: "You can't be mothering in the writing." In other words, I have to resist the urge to protect him, to fluff his résumé, in the stories I tell. The desire I have to make him (and us) look good immediately gums up the narrative and turns the writing soft. I can't protect and reveal at the same time.

Writing is the opposite of mothering.

By craning my neck almost out my office window I can see that he is on the last page. I whip downstairs. He is genial, relaxed, smiling.

"No big problems here," he says, all business. "Just a couple things. Otherwise, good."

I sit down. He thinks I have been fair in my portrayal of our fight at the cottage.

"Maybe take out the phrase 'cold blue eyes'; it makes me sound like a psychopath. And in the chapter when I move back to Toronto, you need to indicate that the tone has changed and I'm not angry."

I make notes. I am impressed. His response to this book about how kids in their twenties are taking their time to grow up and leave home is remarkably mature. Clearly, it's time to stop writing.

■

In most family memoirs, it's traditionally the children who blow the whistle on their parents. Mothers who write fretful magazine articles about their son's online gambling or fathers who publish books about what it's like to live with an autistic child are new. It's clear that the protective silence that used to surround the family has been breached. (In England, Julie Myerson caused a stir with her memoir *The Lost Child*, about her difficult, dope-smoking son. He claims he is not the grim addict she portrays, has publicly called his mother "insane," and hates the book.)

My family is a little offbeat, shall we say, but blessedly free of genuine damage or affliction. No one is in rehab or small-claims court as I write this. I'm only talking about the ordinary anguish of raising normal children in this book—particularly the twilight stage, when they leave home, then come back, then leave again.

3

I wrote my first book, *The Mother Zone*, after having my first (and only) child at the age of 37. I am a bit astonished at my own candour, now that I riffle through it again. My son grew up from birth to the age of eight in the course of the book, and all I had to do was read him the relevant passages and remove one or two that involved bodily functions to acquire his permission to go public. It was obvious to him that writing books was a silly activity, and less fun than drawing.

As for my husband, luckily he is a writer and film critic, some-one who understands the exigencies of storytelling. He didn't mind playing a role in my version of things, even when it wasn't always flattering. A good story, like a long marriage, has to have some conflict.

The Mother Zone was published in 1992, when parenting was still a non-subject. The lusty outback of mothers who blog did not exist—nor did the word "blog"—and my notion that the interior life of a mother was a compelling and unexplored topic was not yet shared by publishers. Still, it felt like a book I had to write.

Eighteen years later, I am surprised to find that it is being read by a new generation of women, as if nothing has changed. Well, that's not true; strollers have evolved. Now they have cup holders, if not GPS. But I'm convinced that despite the new visibility—inescapability, some would say—of the subject, motherhood will always ambush women. It's the great unraveller.

This is because we keep making up new rules to mask the truth of parenthood, which is that raising children is a bottomless and unfixable state of being in love. We're swept along in family like a current. One moment it's exhilarating; we think we've got the hang of it. The next moment our children swirl out of sight, and we panic. Along the way, to deal with the fear of loving and losing our children, each generation creates new myths about motherhood.

For instance, there is this wistful notion that caring for kids is a temporary passage. New parents are shadowed by the expectation that they will, and should, "get back to normal" once the children (a) sleep through the night (b) eat solids (c) go off to college. But whether you embrace it or run away from it, family is forever.

One myth, which must have fuelled more than a few cases of postpartum depression and countless gin and tonics, was that all women love being mothers and are instantly good at it, thanks to a mystery hormone called "maternal instinct." The past two decades of women writing frankly about motherhood have put that one to rest.

More recent myths are that "all mothers are ambivalent and conflicted about their role" and "being an at-home, full-time mother is best for our kids but drives women crazy." Young women now plunge into motherhood armed with information, ready to finesse it, like grad school or a job interview. But parenthood is not just a skill set. Nor is abundant love going to solve all the stuff that family puts in our way. Nobody anticipates the heartache that comes with the *normal* course of things, let alone life plus bad luck.

Three years ago, a publisher asked me if I would consider writing a sequel to *The Mother Zone*. "You must be joking," I said. "My son is 24." Then it struck me that I was in the grip of yet another myth: the empty nest. Although my son was living in another city, he was often back under our roof, and certainly never far from my thoughts. This was a new and growing suburb of the mother zone. And I knew from talking to my friends that many parents of my generation are deeply engaged, if not ensnared, in their grown kids' lives.

The moment I said to my publisher that I wasn't a card-carrying mother any more, I knew it wasn't true. As a mother, I am chronic. It's part of the job description, apparently.

■

Twenty percent of North American children between the ages of 18 and 29 still live with their families. Many are taking their time to find their way. Yet this is slightly embarrassing terrain for parents, our habit of staying awake until the 23-year-old son comes through the door at 3 a.m. or our delicate manoeuvrings to help a daughter snag an internship. We read articles about the listlessness of the "boomerang generation," their entitlement and lack of direction. We don't like to consider how our overparenting may have contributed to this. Or is a long incubation period simply the new face of family?

Helping our children make their way in the world isn't unique to this generation, of course. Long ago sons automatically went into their father's business, whether it was stone masonry or innkeeping; daughters married the boy from the next concession. In fact, it might have been only the boomers who proved the exception, when they rebelled against family values and subscribed to the "generation gap," confident that they could totally re-engineer human beings, capitalism, and music. It was unthinkable to live with our parents after the age of 20 or to work in dad's office. We had better things to do. What, I can't remember.

But now that some of us are hitting 60, the future has narrowed. We see the end. Sure, we're all going to live in funky geriatric communes, where we'll organize euthanasia parties with excellent live music. We still have contributions to make to the world (thinning out our ranks, for starters). But in the meantime, our lifelong, fierce attachment to youth, to changing the world and staying young ourselves, may have found a new focus—our twentysomething kids and what they can become for us.

If there's a new generation gap, I think it's the one between how parents and their grown kids now imagine the future. Getting a liberal arts B.A. and going into the self-employed creative fields, the path I took, now seems as precarious as heading out to sea to catch (non-existent) tuna. The so-called secure professions, in business or finance, are no longer secure. The notion of finding a career that will do you for life and end your days with a pension has become a fairytale. It doesn't matter what you do; it's going to be change and change again from here on in, and we'd better be light on our feet. What sometimes looks like stalling on the part of the young may turn out to be our kids saying no to the things that will no longer carry us forward. And yes to strategies we don't yet recognize.

That is what I think on good days.

■

Writing this book was full of contradictory impulses. I had a strong urge to engineer a good ending for us all, even as I dealt with the death of my parents along the way. At the same time, writing about my son was also a comfort to me, a chance to mutter into my hat and to control the narrative in a way that was impossible, or at least unwise, in real life. I clung, and I let go.

In many ways, the current wave of parents writing candidly about their lives constitutes a new sort of fiction, an alloy of truth, hope, and fallible memory. No parent can write the true story of her own children. Love casts a light on everything that is either too pitiless or too forgiving.

One problem with our family, for instance, has been our closeness. It's just the three of us, and we share a lot in common, especially music. When everyone in the family likes Etta James, it's not so easy to break up.

And then there was the business of trying to get some distance on what was unfolding day by day: almost impossible. As Joan Didion has said, a writer always betrays her subjects, sooner or later. This has nothing to do with whether the portrait is loving or critical; it's the act of putting someone on the page that feels mildly, inescapably treacherous. For me the writing itself was an act of separation that I wasn't prepared for. But my son was a step ahead of me in that department.

7

Leaving

W<small>E WATCHED</small> him disappear into airport security. He walked with his usual bounce, even though he wore a towering backpack, with a pair of sneakers and a water bottle tied to the top. As the opaque glass doors slid shut behind him, he didn't turn around, but I waved anyway. Maybe it was the kind of glass that he could see through on his side, but we couldn't on ours.

Then we drove home in an indefinable state, without saying much. There didn't seem to be anything left to say. I had already had all my feelings about our 20-year-old son dropping out of university to hit the road—or "taking a semester off to travel," as I preferred to call it. I had already been sad, annoyed, alarmed, and finally excited, because that's how he felt about this adventure. He was taking a cheap charter to Las Vegas to "ramble around" the southwest desert. Hitchhiking, alone. Then he thought he'd head south to Mexico for a while.

Mexico is very big, I pointed out.

I reminded him that the era of hitchhiking was long over, and that in 2003 only serial killers and hookers would stand around on some ramp in Nevada. But there was a romance going on. Casey had Woody Guthrie's hoboing and probably Chuck Berry's "Route 66" on his mind.

I gazed out the car window at the floral sculptures along the highway, advertising insurance and pharmaceutical companies. Not the Wild West by a long shot. I told myself that this was perfectly normal, for a 20-year-old to test himself. Boys are going to put themselves in harm's way, one way or another. I tried to think of it as a delayed gap year—the one he probably should have taken after high school, before heading off to university in Montreal, at the still-tender age of 18.

Why do we assume that this is the natural order of things, for boys to leave home at the height of their restlessness, to sit in classrooms for four more years?

Then, in the first week of his first year of a history degree—the official version of why things happen in the world—along came 9/11, and the dominant narrative was blown up. No wonder he was rattled. It didn't help that despite being a good student he had always questioned school, waiting for it to click into focus. That winter he put his shoulder to the wheel. He poured himself into writing ambitious essays then couldn't understand why they came back marked B or B+.

"Try less hard," I suggested. "Just give them what they ask for."

When had I arrived at that sort of advice?

"He's taking a semester off to travel," I explained to friends whose sons were working on MBAs or off digging wells in Africa. A couple of footloose months, I thought, and he'd be back in school, grinding out essays on medieval concepts of time and postcolonialism in Africa.

I knew how useless a B.A. in liberal arts had become. But the parent part of my brain had swollen to such unseemly proportions that I still believed university was the last good daycare, the safest channel to a secure future in our unravelling, unforgiving world.

Promise you'll come back and finish your degree, we both argued, in our mild way.

He didn't say no. But he'd wait 'til he got back to make up his mind.

I did what I could; I went down to Mountain Equipment Co-op and bought him a small, shiny camping stove. A shard of home. He reassured us that he would stay in touch, although not by cellphone. Historically, hobos didn't have cellphones. He would email us from Internet cafés. Every village in Mexico has one, he said.

There were no fights about this, but then conflict has never been our forte. Brian's family is British, and his mother's mantra, to which I aspire, is "Never mind!" Casey has always been civil and tactful with us but firm, as if negotiating with slightly impaired, part-time employees.

So off he went, holding his brown cowboy hat with the curled-up brim—a gift from his gently departing first-year girlfriend. Lindsay was doing an exchange semester abroad, in Hong Kong. Sensible girl!

■

I shouldn't have been surprised by this turn of events. After all, Brian and I had both spent most of our twenties kicking around the world, ignoring the future. But when we left, our parents didn't drive us to the airport, and in those days the generation gap worked like email in reverse: the point was *not* to stay in touch. The technology of the day reinforced the gap, since long-distance phone calls were expensive and the connections were poor; on a call from Burlington to Greece my father's voice sounded like it was coming from the bottom of the ocean (which it was). Airmail letters took forever. They sat scattered around Europe in American Express offices, waiting weeks for us to show up and claim them, if we didn't change our itinerary. And back home, nobody opened the front door to check the mailbox 20 times a day.

Once we left, we were gone. And what our parents didn't know (a great deal, which I will get to) couldn't hurt them.

■

When we got back home, Brian settled back in at the computer, his mind already on other things. I drifted around, picking up odds and ends Casey had left behind in his old room. The McGill calendar, with tick marks beside strange courses—"Soil Science" or "The Physics of Music"—that he was hoping would be more "real" than history. I shoved the wooden case of crumpled tubes of acrylic paint back under his bed. He had the artist gene, all right (from his grandfather), but he probably wasn't going to take that route. Music was more his thing, playing and writing it. Still, it wasn't at all clear what path he was going to choose.

Which is normal, I thought, at 20.

I stowed the emergency-orange rain jacket I had bought him because he was always riding his bike home at 2 a.m. and kept his old address book, slightly curved from being carried in his back jeans pocket. Downstairs, his guitar amp (built decades earlier by my brother) was still set up in the dining room. I wound the power cable around the handle and lugged the TV-sized amp down into the basement. No more home recordings for now.

A few days later, we got our first message, a group email to family and friends:

Date: Tue, 17 Feb 2003 12:46:32 -0500
Subject: New Mexico

Hi there,

I am in Santa Fe and alive and well. Nevada, Arizona, and New Mexico are beautiful! I spent my first night sleeping behind the "Welcome to Las Vegas" sign beside the airport. Planes are loud. Vegas is bright all the time. Then I spent the whole next day trying to get out of town.

Hitchhiking to Zion National Park was not successful. Word to the wise, do not try to hitch out of Vegas and into Utah—bad combination . . .

"Sounds like he's doing all right," Brian remarked.

"What are you saying?" I yelped, face in my hands. "Our son just spent the night sleeping on the ground, behind the 'Welcome to Las Vegas' sign!"

"He'll survive. Casey's resourceful."

The details came later. He had gotten off the plane thinking he could find a hostel or perhaps a grassy ditch to camp in. But Vegas is not a town of grassy ditches. He took buses all over, looking for the university ("students, they live cheaply"), then a hostel, then a cheap motel. But even the Super 8 on the outskirts of town cost an exorbitant $90. So, still wearing his overstuffed pack and cowboy hat, carrying his guitar, he made his way back to the airport, where he found a semi-secluded patch of grass behind the "Welcome" sign. He brushed his teeth and unrolled his sleeping bag. Not wanting to draw attention to himself, he decided not to put up his tent.

Desert nights, he discovered, can be surprisingly cold. In the morning, he made his way to the outskirts of the city, where he stood by the side of the road for five hours without getting a ride. Then he went back into town and bought a bus ticket to Santa Fe.

Just when you think your job as a mother is on the wane, the circuits all light up again.

■

In second year, before he dropped out, Casey had moved into an apartment with four roommates, a vast, Montreal-sized flat around the corner from the bagel shop on St. Viateur. It was sunny, with an old porcelain kitchen sink that hit you mid-thigh and a back balcony full of drying laundry and bicycles. The smell of grilled lamb and oregano from the Greek restaurant around the corner drifted in the windows. The apartment was a block away from the bohemian scene on the patio of the Club Social and across the street from a crepe shop where one of his roommates worked, pouring batter onto a grill the size of a record turntable. Ground Zero in Mile End, maybe the coolest intersection in North America for someone his age (or so it seemed to me). But he had decided that he would rather fly to the southwestern States in the dying days of that empire, to stand in the middle of the desert with this thumb out.

Did we play too much Dylan? Was it the cover of *Bringing It All Back Home* staring out at the three of us, that woman in the red dress? Even though we didn't mythologize the past, our cultural debris was still lying around, and Casey seemed to have inherited some of our creaky old cynicism about "the system." Careers were for squares. He had no time for the go-getters, the ones climbing the ladder. He was an outlaw; he would make his own way.

Wrong era, I felt like telling him. That romance is over. Even the phrase "dropping out" had been our idea, back when *not* working was the most ambitious thing you could do. In 1969 spending time in Tangiers was tantamount to getting an MBA. We did finish our degrees, but school was a relatively carefree experience, not the angsty job-grooming factory it has since become. The culturally approved thing for someone growing up then was to get as far from family as possible and to inhale the world.

And that was how we spent the next 10 years or so, fomenting revolution and playing in a band (Brian) or travelling, falling in love, and occasionally writing (me). Postponing adulthood, certainly. Alarming our families.

In many ways, we had simply conformed to the times. But it was obvious from our photo albums and our modest capital assets— we were in our thirties before we could commit to buying a couch, let alone a house—that we had valued freedom and adventure over careers and financial security. Because when we were growing up, that luxurious range of options still existed.

Now, our desire to reinvent the world has dwindled for many of us to a spirited defence of our right to unpasteurized cheese. But a familiar flame of indignation burned on in Casey. In school he was impatient just reading "one guy's version of what happened in the past"; he wanted to get out into the world, to see and feel it for himself.

I saw his point. I had done the same thing, after all. But I also didn't want him to lose his place in the fearful queue of training and competition that had become his culture.

■

My parents were the first generation in their modest prairie families to go to university, in Saskatoon. Education meant a great deal to them, but they didn't pressure me to go to college. I could always work as a secretary. Or I could teach. (I was 40 before she threw out my old high-school textbooks, imagining they might come in handy the day I came to my senses and enrolled in teachers' college.) University was more of a finishing-school, where girls went to get a smattering of knowledge while meeting "husband material." My father encouraged my "flair for words" urging me to "write something funny for *Reader's Digest*" (which I have only recently accomplished). So I ambled my way through an English degree, which suited me fine.

But I don't think my parents and I ever had a single conversation about what I might "become." I was a girl; I already was who I was going to be.

That was then. Now, however, there have been endless conversations with my son, wearying to both of us, about what he might "become." And all my alarms and doubts about this process were, unoriginally, funnelled into the question of school. If only he had gone to that cozy alternative school instead of the downtown public school he preferred. Or private school. Et cetera. Like Effexor, I thought school was the pill my son could swallow to solve our anxiety around what his true place in the world should be.

But maybe school wasn't the culprit. Maybe it was the cultural stuff he grew up around, all the romantic outlaws who sang and wrote about the American dream, when there still was one. I wandered into Casey's old room to do some forensics.

His bed faced a wall of bookshelves, full of our old heroes, half-mad visionaries like R. D. Laing and Charles Bukowski, ambitious Sylvia Plaths and train-hopping Al Purdys glaring down at him while he slept. Our books line one entire wall in "his" room, from the floor to the ceiling, but as I sat there I remembered the bookcase that Casey had kept in our previous house, as a teenager. It was just two shelves long, but strenuously edited. In a household full of print, with two journalist parents, he claimed not to be a reader. At 14 and 15, though, he did surreptitiously read, with his full attention. I could still reconstruct the titles that he kept in his room:

— Woody Guthrie, *Bound for Glory*
— George Orwell, *Down and Out in Paris and London*
— *Catcher in the Rye*, by J.D. Salinger, of course (Brian handed it to him in a bookstore when he was 14; he opened the maroon-covered paperback, read the first few lines and said, "I'll take this one.")
— *Franny and Zooey*
— Jack Kerouac, *On the Road*
— A couple early stories by John Steinbeck, I forget which.
— Hunter S. Thompson, *Fear and Loathing in Las Vegas*
— Al Purdy, *Rooms to Rent in the Outer Planets*
— Bob Dylan, *Chronicles*. No, that came out later.

I forgot Allen Ginsberg's *Howl*. Casey's copy had migrated back onto our shelves, where the spine caught my eye. It was an original $3.95 City Lights edition, published in 1956. I opened to the first page, where Ginsberg begins his catalogue of "angelheaded hipsters" and the ones "who disappeared into the volcanoes of Mexico"—oh dear—"leaving behind nothing but the shadow of dungarees and the lava and ash of poetry scattered in fire-place Chicago. . . ."

Dungarees. A beautiful word fallen out of use.

I closed it. If only Casey had read less, not more.

Date: Sat, 28 Feb 2003 00:15:32 -0500
Subject: Buenos Dias

Hello from between Silver City and Truth or Consequences, New Mexico.

Here is the latest news from my southwestern adventures. I've been staying in a place called the Mimbers Valley, in the mountains of south-central New Mexico, about a hundred miles north of the border. My hosts are Eric and Nancy, who run a pinhole photography journal and supplies business. I hitched here from Santa Fe on Saturday and got rides from all sorts of people . . .

The email went on to describe his conversations with Bill, a Vietnam vet from Georgia ("excellent company"), a video-editor dude, and José from Durango. José and his truck took him over the mountains into the Mimbers Valley as he quizzed Casey at some length about his personal relationship with Jesus.

Later he stopped and got me to take some photos of him posed in front of the truck with the mountains. He didn't seem to mind that I hadn't found Jesus. He was more surprised that I didn't have a cellphone.

New Mexico is wild and woolly. I've met a guy from Vancouver who lives in a 100 percent vegetable oil-fuelled truck. I've heard such statements as "We were building the camera obscura when Maggie, the emu, got into the concrete and ate half a bag of it. But she was fine."

Now I am heading in the direction of Oaxaca, Mexico, via Las Cruces, El Paso, Juarez and many buses.

Hasta la vista,
Casey

Another email made a casual reference to "maybe hopping freights." Okay, hitchhike if you must, I zinged back, but do us a favour: no freight trains. Yes, it's the hipster street-cred thing to do. But people also get their legs chopped off, I reminded him. Railyard guard dogs can bite you, and security will arrest you. He was noncommittal in his reply.

One of the songs he liked to sing, I remembered, was Springsteen's version of a ballad by Woody Guthrie:

The highway is alive tonight
But nobody's kiddin' nobody about where it goes
I'm sittin' down here in the campfire light
Searchin' for the ghost of Tom Joad

■

Like many other families of our generation, Casey is an only child who moved easily among adults and our community of friends. The three of us could all sit on the couch and laugh at *This Is Spinal Tap*, and we were a good example, I thought, of the sort of modern family where the kids don't rebel and parental roles blur into a kind of peer friendship with our children. Which we enjoyed, of course; Casey is great company, full of energy, and funny. His ease in our circles, with roots in the old days when community was more important than making money, seemed like a good thing. But there was no confusing our fading world with the one coming up.

My parents and their attention to the art of "home" also impressed him. His grandfather was an engineer whose practical skills represented a refreshing switch from our own two-writer jerry-rigged household. My mother was a knowledgeable and inventive cook who liked to track her grandson's quixotic appetites and allergies. When Casey went vegan for a few years in his teens, my mother rose to the challenge of pigs in a blanket, hold the blanket, hold the pig. He and my mother share a certain mad-scientist creativity.

What I didn't realize when our son first left home was that the leaving had only begun. The dramas, conflict, and heartbreaks were still to come, in the course of his early twenties, as we kept negotiating and renegotiating our closeness, our distance. At the age of 18 his values were admirable, if somewhat untested. He believed in treating others with fairness and respect, and he couldn't abide anyone in authority who abused their power. But he wasn't grown up yet, not by a long shot. And we still had ground to cover as parents.

In the meantime, it didn't matter to Casey that the Summer of Love was now just a vintage T-shirt or that the world has since become a more venal and dangerous place than the one I travelled through. He thought I was just catastrophizing as usual.

Another issue, minor but genuine, was that I didn't *want* him to be disappointed by Chuck Berry or Woody Guthrie. I wanted the songs and the books to be true.

19

Vertical Travel

I N M Y E F F O R T S not to fret about him, I told myself that Casey had embarked on something that boys his age seem to hunger after, in one form or another: a rite of passage; a journey, preferably dangerous, to carry them over the threshold from boyhood to manhood. In aboriginal cultures (what is left of them), these ceremonies still take place. The circumstances are important. If possible, they unfold in a natural setting, in the company of elders, on hallowed ancestral ground.

In my son's case, spending his first night on the road sleeping under the "Welcome to Las Vegas" sign might have been the closest thing his culture has to offer as sacred ground.

Traditionally, a rite of passage involves some sort of physical deprivation or test: a fast, a sweat lodge session, a night spent alone in the wilderness (or all three). Other elements might contribute to a state of altered consciousness—the burning of sweet grass, chanting, dancing, or drumming. It's an opportunity for a young man to test his strength and courage, within the protective circle of a wider clan, in a ceremony that marks his coming of age in body, soul, and mind.

(For many boys in western culture, I suppose the equivalent ritual is the march across a stage wearing a robe and a flat black hat to show their courage in the face of higher education.)

In aboriginal cultures, a boy on the brink of manhood is in a liminal, threshold state, both precarious and profound. According to anthropologist Arnold van Gennep, there are three stages associated with liminality and rite of passage: separation from the community, transformation, and finally reintegration into society in a renewed role. For our city-bred, digital boys we seem to have finessed the separation stage. There is a tendency to treat them as a separate benighted species. But the transformative part remains elusive, and reintegration into society—i.e., growing up—is protracted, if not off the agenda entirely.

The pencil marks on the wall keep inching upward as we track maturity. Twenty-five is not just the new 20; some social scientists, through a mysterious calibration, now put the onset of adulthood at 31. Neuroscience suggests that young brains aren't really "cooked" until around age 25 (something to keep in mind when 14-year-olds smoke industrial-strength weed). Everyone's lifespan has also increased, which spreads maturity across a wider arc. In short, youth lasts longer now. Sometimes it seems as if the entire culture is wearing its baseball cap backwards, at any age. (One hundred is the new two?)

Instead of being a brief stage, for many young men the liminal state—being betwixt and between, at risk, on the cusp, unlaunched—stretches over a period years. Our response often doesn't help the situation; parents see the hallmarks of adolescence as flaws to be fixed, not as a process unfolding. Rather than accepting this period of doubt and confusion as part of growing up and learning courage, we ride them to get it together. Their response is to retreat further inside the treehouse of adolescence, where we aren't welcome. Which is fine with us. Boys will be boys. Separation from society is just what we expect from them.

■

Date: Mon, 15 Mar 2003 17:11
Subject: Hello from Chiapas

Here are a few exciting facts from Mexico . . .

Buses come in all shapes and sorts. Most have something at the front
for good luck, like the Virgin of Guadalupe, Jesus, a saint maybe or Bob
Marley. Whatever gets you down the road. The chocolate is great here.
The markets are also great. Every imaginable cow part. Live chickens
and pigs on leashes. Mounds of grasshoppers. It's all about the flesh
and blood around here.

And, Family. People are so sad that I have no brothers or sisters. Just
yesterday, riding with a family in the back of their pickup, one of the
kids asked me if I was married, if I had kids, and was rather worried
that I wasn't and didn't . . .

■

Well, maybe he had to go all the way to Mexico to get some good
news about family life. I was sorry he had to have his epiphanies by
himself, on the fly, but he didn't seem to mind being on his own.

Although the rite of passage experience traditionally unfolds
in the company of the older generation, it clears a space for a boy
to venture down into himself, and to encounter himself alone.
It's a chance for a boy to flex his autonomy within the respectful
embrace of his clan, and another way of being on the road—a
form of vertical travel.

For many men, joining the military or going off to war is
the closest they will come to a rite of passage that lets them bond
with other men and test their courage. It's certainly a good way to
split off from society. But reintegration is more elusive. For some
soldiers who have been through the horrors of combat, there is

no true coming home. Friends and family don't understand what they've been through. It's easy for these combat-traumatized 19- and 20-year-olds to end up stalled in a liminal state, exiled from their past and yet unable to step into the future.

No wonder growing up lacks appeal, for civilians and soldiers alike, given the dismal associations adulthood has acquired. It needs to be rebranded so we don't see it as the rather boring part that comes between youth and death. We don't see dying as something inevitable at the far end of a natural continuum; instead it's kept apart like a snake in a box, under lock and key.

Our fear of aging and death doesn't register directly on the young, of course. Twenty-year-old boys don't go around saying, "Dying scares me therefore I am going to skateboard forever." But adulthood seems to involve certain penalties: marriage as a loss of masculine freedom; "settling down" as giving up on your dreams; growing up as a diminishment of spirit and energy. Adulthood arrives with a shadow of compromise and capitulation instead of a sense of expansion, adventure, or growth in wisdom and stature.

In the past, aboriginal cultures haven't shared this way of thinking. They revered their elders and respected their experience. Of course, around the world these cultures are losing the traditional ways, and the role of their elders has become as endangered as their languages. In western culture, the old are seen as largely powerless, burdensome, and silly. Look at Homer Simpson's addled dad (look at Homer, for that matter). Why *should* a boy grow up, if that's what's in store?

So the threshold period in a young man's life drags on longer and longer. Rite-of-passage behaviour consumes years, even decades, and revolves around social rituals that involve plenty of risk but little renewal, such as binge-drinking, now entrenched among the young, not to mention much of the adult world.

But consider all the pressures on twentysomethings to "become" something—to get the degree, settle on a "career path," score an entry-level job, find the right mate. That's a long to-do list. There is pressure, in other words, to be anything *but* what you are, at 22 or 23, which is very often alone and in flux, if not in chaos. No wonder getting wrecked is so popular. Community on the Internet is also liminality defined, a constant state of in-betweenness and flux. Twitter as sweat lodge. It's all good, from the neck up. But the integration of mind, body, and spirit is hard to come by in cyberspace.

Apart from encountering a good philosophy prof, there's little that encourages or rewards a young man for actively questioning the world he is expected to join. If our sons are feeling lost, their searching and their doubts alarm us. Nobody says to them, "Don't worry. Confusion isn't failure or weakness. This is part of it. Just sit with yourself for a while and learn." We confuse liminal with limbo.

But before careers and family responsibilities come into the picture, there are a few undefined years of vulnerability that offer a chance to come to grips with who you are. Tough work at 23 or 53.

And with questing boys, things can also end badly. When I saw the movie *Into the Wild*, I was a wreck before the opening credits had even ended, for two reasons: Emile Hirsch bears a spooky resemblance to Casey in his high-haired period; and having read Jon Krakauer's book, I knew the outcome of this particular rite of passage. The main character's desire to cut loose from school and family, to experience the land, was so close to my son's impulse to roam the American deserts. The hero's attempt to shed the "system" and live in the wild was appealing but he was also naïve and underestimated the risks involved. He left behind his family as well as the friends he had made on the road to spend the winter alone, in a remote part of Alaska. He set up camp in an abandoned school bus. There, just as he came to realize that he missed people and wanted to rejoin society, he made one small mistake. He ate the wrong plant, got sick, and slowly died.

It's a fine movie, but I wish I hadn't seen it. Especially the scenes where an old guy befriends the hero just before he embarks on his wilderness sojourn. The old man offers to adopt him as his son. The scene where this loving elder drops him off and watches him head off into the bush in borrowed boots is the point where rite of passage turns into youthful folly.

And the young still need us.

■

By heading down into the American desert on his own, my son had opted for the classic liminal elements of solitude and independence, along with a measure of danger and discomfort. But there was no wider clan to protect and observe him, or to welcome him back into the fold. Well, there was his tiny family, loving, WASPy, unclannish clan that we are. And there were one or two family friends along his route to visit with and cook him dinner. But no older figures shadowing him into the future. His father was back home, assuming that all would be well with his wandering son—because he had wandered too as a young man, taken risks, and survived. Then there was me, firing off emails to him about level 60 sunscreen and highway bandits. Useful advice. But for a 20-year-old, useful advice from your mother is the last thing you want.

The other missing component of his trip was the survival of ancestral ground and an intact culture of his own. He was travelling in pre-Obama America, a country that had been in deep decay for some time. The Wild West that Casey had envisioned, that Chuck Berry sang about, Dylan's fabled Highway 61 or the small towns that Springsteen mythologizes, were not so easy to locate.

"I now realize that in America, you're nobody if you don't have a car," he emailed us one day. "When I stand on the on-ramp, people throw $2 bills at me out of the car windows as they go by. And not in a friendly way."

■

We don't seem to know what to do with our boys. They get wasted, and we waste them. It's hard to pay attention to young men in ways that take them seriously, physically challenge them, and delight in their boyness. Everything boyish—wildness, exuberance, defiance, frail pride, and restlessness—becomes a potential deficit in our eyes. We overparent them and underestimate them, and our anxiety only registers as a lack of faith.

So boys improvise. They come together in skateboard parks or hockey rinks, dance clubs, abandoned buildings, underpasses. They walk over fiery coals of their own invention. They burn. We are clumsy in our guidance. And some of the lost ones come back to us stronger than the lucky, rare ones who glide through young manhood unscathed.

■

It was now March, the worst month of all if you live in Toronto. Winter recedes like the tide going out on a beach, revealing all the debris and orphaned bits that the snow has covered up. The wind has a bitter edge.

Another email arrived from Casey in southern Mexico, advising us not to eat an entire papaya at one sitting. "I don't know why, but it is a bad feeling," he reported. He had had a music session with some locals who were passing around a guitar.

"*They keep asking me to play* Besame Mucho, *but that never works. But I get a very warm reception for Johnny Cash and Janis Joplin. And it's true, everyone loves the Beet-les. They have this great chocolate drink here, called atole. . . .*"

I had forgotten that part: it's fun to be footloose in another country. Perhaps what I needed was a rite of passage of my own—

a trip out of my chronic state of motherhood and on to some fresher version of myself. Or back to a former one. I began looking into flights to some place warm. Apart from Mexico.

It turned out that the cheapest fares flew to the Algarve, in southern Portugal. This happened to be a country I travelled through in my twenties, on my own. There was a romance involved too, with someone I had met on the road. I still kept a stash of his letters in my office.

So when I came across a listing for a charter flight and an apartment in a mountain village not far from my old haunts, I booked them both. A solo trip might remind me of how normal and benign life on the road can be. At the very least, it might pry me off email.

Brian endorsed my getaway, a bit too enthusiastically I thought. Maybe we all needed a break from family.

The Road

T THE FARO AIRPORT, I step out into the soft, bright
early morning air, where Brenda, the agent I had found online, is waiting for me. She's my age, short and robust. A
few years ago, fed up with the winters in Dorset, she moved to a village near Alte, where she lives alone with her corgis in a renovated
church.

Hmm. Is this my new template? Other women I know are heading off to treks in Bhutan or ashrams in India. Instead I'm going
to drive a rental car around a place I've already been, famous for
olives and unbearably sad music, while I try not to worry about
my son.

I grip the wheel of my navy blue Corsa and follow Brenda's
SUV along the expressways and roundabouts of Faro as the roads
circle, ascend, narrow, and then deteriorate. My eyes want to shut;
they think it should be night. We climb away from the coast with
its high-rises and golf courses into the sparsely populated hills—
dry, brown, rugged mountains, worn down like molars, domesticated by centuries of farming. Not Canada, raw and unauthored.

As we drive north, I think about the turn life had taken on my
first flight to Portugal, in 1971. I was 25.

■

We were in the "smoking section" of the plane, a conceptual corral marked by an imaginary line through the airspace of the cabin. I rummaged around for my blue packet of Drum tobacco and rolled him one too. We smoked our cigarettes and talked some more, about Neil Young, Günter Grass and Hermann Hesse. He seemed smart and charmingly jaded for his age, the same as mine. Then we went back to reading. Elbows touching.

I had spotted him in the check-in line; his hair was long and blond like mine, only more ragged, and he wore purple bell-bottoms frayed at the hem, a white Indian shirt, and mirror aviator shades. The more dandyish style of the London hippie, with a whiff of old money too, perhaps. I was wearing a rose-coloured shirt from Biba's and a patchwork vest I had made out of scraps of my old clothes, including the bad turquoise prom dress and the lining from my mother's fur coat.

I contrived to sit beside him on the plane. It turned out that he had worked as a journalist in London, although he was already disenchanted with the scene.

"A seedy lot, when you get down to it," he said. I didn't mention that I earned my living, such as it was, writing book reviews for a newspaper.

When we landed in Lisbon, there was an awkward stretch as we left the plane and I didn't know whether to walk beside him. Passengers rushing to make their connections jostled around us. As we came to a Y in the corridors he turned to me.

"You're staying a while in Lisbon, then?"

"Yeah, at the hostel. I'll check out the city for a few days, then probably hitchhike south to Sagres."

He gestured up the other arm of the hall. "I've got to catch my flight, but if you end up in the area, come find me. I'm staying in the hills north of Faro, near São Brás de Alportel. Ask after the *inglês* in the village; anyone will tell you the way."

I tried to memorize the name of the village, but the slurry Portuguese syllables were new to me.

He started walking down the corridor then turned.

"Alportel, not Albufeira," he called back. "You don't want to go there."

"Don't worry, I won't!" I sang out. Then he was gone.

Chris was his name. Chris who?

■

Now the roads have turned into glossy cobblestones, and Brenda and I must drive slowly. The village of Santa Margarita turns out to be nothing more than a cluster of whitewashed houses and one church, perched on the saddle between a pair of mountains. We find the Rua Dos Corralloes (where there actually is a corral, with two grey horses). The lane narrows between high white walls until it is barely wider than my car mirrors, and we arrive at my *casita* for one.

Not bad, I think, for an Internet stab in the dark: a pretty white house like the others in the village, with dark green shutters and a scalloped, orange-tiled roof. The familiar rooster-shaped weather vane. Brenda hands over the keys and drives off—rather quickly, I notice, as if I might change my mind and race back to the airport. I suppose it is odd, a middle-aged woman on her own holed up here in March, before the blossoms are out. The place has the sequestered aspect I remember from my first time in the Algarve, with the houses facing inward to walled courtyards. As if winds and hot sun are bad spirits.

I stand in the driveway and look south over a gentle green slope of orchards, still tight-budded, across broad scrubby plains to a thin, silver line flashing on the horizon—the sea. The owners, who live in the apartment across the courtyard, don't seem to be home. An invisible donkey brays, but otherwise it's silent.

I jerk my suitcase wheels over the cobblestones and roll it into the bedroom, where the bed is high and puffy. A sizable brown spider scuttles out of the corner, and I accidentally roll over it. Oh dear, bad juju. I bounce on the bed. Here I am, apparently the only tourist on this mountain in southern Portugal, at the end of a cobbled road in off-season. It's much cooler than I expected.

Car wheels crunch in the driveway, and I hurry out to meet the owners, a short, energetic East Indian woman and her partner, a shy New Zealander with a snaggle-toothed smile. Bob and Kathy. I like them immediately. They open the shutters and doors of my apartment to let the sun in. What about phones and computers, I quiz them. They do have a computer, but it is dial-up and unreliable. The nearest hotel, a half hour's drive away, might have an Internet connection for guests, but they aren't sure. As for telephones, there's a kiosk in Alte, another half hour beyond the hotel.

"This is why people come here," Kathy says, smiling, "to be out of touch."

Interestingly, I have travelled to a corner of the developed world where communication with my family will be more problematic than from the smallest village of Mexico.

Now it's my son's turn to find me.

■

The next morning, I consider an exploratory tramp around the valley. Little birds are singing in the courtyard. Instead, I drive directly to the neo-Grecian, deserted-looking hotel on the road to Alte. A computer the size of a convection oven sits idle in a spare office, and for a Euro they let me use it. After many pings and gurgles the thing dredges up the Internet, like a squid in a fishing net. I log in and find a fresh email from Casey.

Date: Mon, 15 Mar 2003 17:11:24 -0500
Subject: Hello from Chiapas

Yesterday, I played soccer with a bunch of Jehovah's Witnesses, who referred to me as Canada. "Hey Canada, aqui, aqui!" And not one word about Jesus.

I am considering buying this Brooklyn dude's bike and touring gear to bike around Guatemala and Chiapas, but we'll see. I am in the mountain city of San Cristobal de las Casas now, which is full of tourists, but also is still great and old.

I have been asked to "Say hi to Comandante Marcos" from a guy in Salina Cruz, but I don't plan on taking up arms. In any case, people love the revolution here. Next stop is either Guatemala or back up the Caribbean coast.

Great! *Comandante Casey*. What could be more appealing to a boy fed up with middle-class Toronto? I review the available options: either he will join the Zapatistas or he will bicycle alone through Guatemala, where the Canadian Embassy is now posting daily warnings for tourists.

His email goes on to say that he plans to meet up with the cycle dude after a few weeks, in Guatemala, near Lake Atitlan. They'll rendezvous in a town called Panajachel.

Panajachel! This time I know exactly what is in store for him, and at last I have a legitimate reason to worry. As it happens—I don't think Casey even knows or remembers this about his mother—I rode a bicycle through Guatemala when I was in my twenties. And it was the road leading up from Panajachel that almost did me in. You climb 2,000 vertical feet on a grade that would cause a donkey to tip over. It's stupid. But it's just a vague plan, I thought, and maybe it will fall through. He doesn't like to plan.

I leave the hotel and head back to my casita, where I pour a giant glass of Vinho Verde and ponder the ironies of my situation. Now I know—exactly—how my parents must have felt when I told them that I was going to bike my way down into South America with Tom ("The one with the motorcycle?" my father asked). I remember the day I took the commuter train home to Burlington to break the news.

■

It was late November. The first flakes of snow were whirling around in a dither, as if to say, "Where the hell are we—isn't there some place nicer we can land?" The air had that stony cold that arrives just in time for the Santa Claus parade.

34

I stepped off the train to my father's waiting car. The front seat of the big Buick was covered in a woolly sheepskin, and so was the steering wheel; the circulation in his fingers was poor, and his hands got cold. We drove home, where my mother was still in her blue bathrobe, sitting in the den. This was unheard of in the middle of the afternoon. She didn't get up to greet me, she just swivelled in my direction, looking filmy-eyed and distant—the Valium look. She was sitting in her usual spot, an upholstered chair (everything in our house was upholstered, including the placemats) that rocked and pivoted. She liked to sit there and watch the kids walk home from my old school, a few blocks away.

Earlier that fall, after several days of feeling flu-ish and weak, she had slowly walked the two blocks to Dr. Bodkin's office.

"I think I'm having a heart attack," she politely informed the receptionist.

She spent about a week in the hospital and then came home to recover. I'm not even sure my father informed me of the details; in those days, a woman's heart attack didn't have the drama of a masculine cardiac event. Years later, I wondered if it might not have been an episode of depression, or a bit of both; it hadn't been a good year for my mother. My 20-year-old sister had just married, had a baby, and moved to Toronto, out from under her wing. My brother's first marriage was rocky. The whole family was unravelling, and now I was heading off too, on some cockamamie trip with boyfriend C, or D, when I should be signing up for teachers' college.

None of the usual dips and zero-fat snacks awaited me in the kitchen. I made a pot of tea and gave them both a spirited pitch about the value and legitimacy of this new adventure of mine. Tom and I would be part of a group, a National Geographic expedition, I pointed out. (Briefly. We decided to fly over the impenetrable Darien Gap and make our own way down through South America.) I would learn Spanish (the words for "inner tube" and "severe diarrhea"). Using my mother's old sewing machine, I had already made some flare-orange bike panniers from a mail-order kit. And look, I said, we cut up our map and glued it to a big piece of cloth, so it can be folded and refolded without ripping.

They glanced at the huge map, with our route inked in black, and said nothing. To my prairie-raised parents, South America was unimaginable, a lawless continent of anacondas and piranhas. (We did in fact encounter a very, very, very long anaconda, the diameter of a telephone pole, sunbathing on a culvert under a bridge. Parents are not always wrong.)

But I wasn't ready to think about my mother as being frail or needing my care. And was it my fault that all three of her kids were not thriving in the ways she had hoped they would? As for being in shape for pedalling through the Andes, that didn't concern me. I had already cut down to one cigarette a day.

"I better go or I'll miss my train," I said, as I stood at the front door with my backpack on, trying not to bump into the door chimes. My mother didn't get up. I leaned over to kiss her, but she seemed to want the moment to pass quickly, so I let it.

"I'll stay in touch and phone at Christmas," I promised. "I can always fly back, you know." She swung back to the window. My father jingled the change in his trouser pocket, a sign that he was agitated. He clamped a hand on my shoulder.

"You be careful down there," he said gruffly, full of love.

■

Back in Santa Margarita, I write postcards while Bob and Kathy water the pots of geraniums in the courtyard, bowing again and again, like monks. The little swimming pool has been filled but it's still too cold to use. I'm considering a quick trip into Alte to buy a bottle of wine and to use the phone kiosk there. It's red, and right in the middle of the main square, like a religious shrine. My outings on this holiday, I realize, are mostly communication-related.

But I know Brian won't be waiting to hear from me. He's probably relieved to have his hand-wringing wife off the grid for a while. At a certain point anxiety becomes more about the anxious one than the object of worry. I know it's only normal for a mother to fret about a young son on the road but I suspect that Casey's going away has also stirred ancient fears in me, of loss and desertion. I can't stop imagining all the terrible things that could happen to the people I love. But then my father was a catastrophizer too.

I remember sitting in the sofa-sized back seat of the Buick when I was young, with my father at the wheel, his big square hands at the ten and two o'clock position. He was driving up the main street, under a yellow traffic light suspended over the road. It swayed slightly in the wind.

"That sort of thing shouldn't be allowed," my father muttered. "It could come crashing down and kill someone." He loved the words "bashing" and "crashing" and used them often, with relish. The weather worried him too, which was not surprising for someone who grew up under unpredictable prairie skies and had lost his own father to TB at the age of 12. He'd stand at the window, twitching the protective curtains (two layers, nylon sheers under heavy pleated drapes, on tracks).

"Look at those clouds," he'd say darkly. "Boy, we're in for it now."

My father was both a worrier and an engineer, which might explain why he became such a consummate fixer of things, a saver, and a planner. What a provider—quaint word!—he was. He would meticulously chart the vicissitudes of the stock market on hand-drawn coloured graphs, copy, laminate, and bind the pages, then present them to his three children. We would thank him and stick the envelopes in a bottom drawer. Money didn't interest us.

■

I walk down into the village, where there isn't a soul in the streets. Is it Sunday? What the hell do they *do* behind those fringed plastic curtains? I pass the sunny patio of a café, where six or seven grizzled men in dark fedoras sit at tables with glasses of *aguardiente*, arguing. It sounds as if they are about to rip each other apart, but it's just an animated conversation. No women in the bars. They stay inside. In their kerchiefs and hats, covered in black from top to toe, they could be wearing hijab. It's a perfect place for a middle-aged woman to feel comfortably invisible.

The café overlooks a broad, lush valley covered in orange groves. Fresh from the sparrow greys of Toronto in March, the oranges look unnatural to me, almost digital. Someone has Photoshopped them in.

The walk back to my street of the two horses is steep, and on the way I glimpse secretive, alluring lanes that curve up, crest, and then disappear out of sight. Everything here seems to happen offstage. The donkey I never see begins to bray, a sound like a strangled sob. It is a hillier version of the landscape I remember from my months with Chris, in Alportel; I take out my maps and see that it's not so far away, to my old haunts. But it feels too soon to go there.

■

THE ROAD

When I get online the next morning, I check the Canadian Embassy website again. I see that new warnings have been posted about bandits and growing political unrest in Guatemala. "Visitors are advised to stay on the main highways and travel during daylight."

I email Casey, in pleading caps:

MI HIJO,
IT IS FOOLISH TO BICYCLE ALONE IN THOSE MOUNTAINS RIGHT NOW. TRUST ME, I KNOW WHAT I'M TALKING ABOUT HERE . . .

Then I log off and force myself to go hiking through the countryside, along the footpaths that once joined the villages. German tourists like to come to this area to "tramp," and so I follow an insanely detailed German walking guide. *You will reach a discarded washing machine beside a wall of bougainvillea; turn left and go 235 metres to a pile of red rocks . . .*

Total physical exhaustion, I find, is helpful. I eat a large plate of grilled sardines and hundreds of green peas then fall into a stupor on my puffy bed. The following day, my very best girlfriend at the Alte hotel smiles and waves me toward the computer, where a fresh email is waiting. Casey has now bought the bike and the touring gear, he reports, and has set off on his trip.

. . . I biked my first day in the direction of Mexico out of Panajachel (they call it gringo town). This happened to be up a mountain that is the rim of the former crater. I wanted to cry, and puke and die. It was a bad first day, accompanied by increasing stomach problems. Around noon, I took a siesta under a tree.

He went on to describe a lone farmer who came along, commiserated with him, and made him an offer; for a few quetzals, he would pray for Casey.

I didn't have small change, and I didn't really want him to pray for me (although it may have helped, in retrospect).

The next day, he was too sick to ride. A pastor in a truck eventually stopped by the side of the road to give him and his bike a lift. Once he had recovered, there was a beautiful three-hour downhill ride from San Marcos, he wrote. Then came the gratifying part:

Biking alone in the mountains of Guatemala was great, but way too hard! Do not try to bike out of Lake Atitlan. It is stupid. The border town of Tapachula is really damn hot too. I felt like my body was going to explode.

■

In Santa Margarita, there's not much to do in the evenings except read and write in my journal.

A cool twilight, with a blustery wind and dark clouds coming. I feel more settled, now that it's almost time to go home. I have my pictures of Casey and Brian, both looking so handsome, propped up in front of me, against my bowl of oranges—the market man gave them to me for free. They're all over the ground here, like rubbish. My gas-fire heater splutters and flutters behind me.

I read a few more of Chris's letters. They're very tender, both toward me and toward our Portuguese neighbours on the hill, Snr. Mario and Sra. Vitoria. An older couple who befriended us. He and Snr. Mario became partners in a hog-raising venture sometime after I left. In one of his letters Chris tells the story of an afternoon he spent drinking with Snr. Mario and a few other men down at the taverna. How, after several copinhos, *the men would improvise little rhyming songs about the wine, or that particular day. One was about how time ran backwards there. O tempo volta para tras.*

I know I've constructed a romance about it all since then,
but why not? There was a man in a white house on a hill, in a
peaceful world, where time ran backward. I could have stayed
to see what would happen, but I moved on instead. As we
tended to in those days.

■

I spoke to Brian on the phone, who finally sounded a bit forlorn. He's having trouble sleeping, he said. He needs that warm back and whirring early-morning brain beside him.

Last night was cold; I slept under two big duvets. My watch has lost its little turner and (tellingly) is stuck on Toronto time. I take out the latest alarming email from Casey and reread it. I didn't quite take it in the first time through:

Date: Wed, 31 Mar 2003 15:36
Subject: Hello from Puebla

Hi there
I spent a week in San Cristobal, the beautiful, tourist-filled, mountain city in Chiapas. I soon found out that ever since the Zapatistas took the city in '94, San Cristobal has been at the centre of the uprising. My first day there, I went to see a movie on the Zapatistas and asked someone if they were here to fight the revolution. I soon learned that you shouldn't really talk about working with Zapatistas in public places—it's better to talk about hiking and visiting churches. So, I saw a bunch of movies on Zapatistas, La Violencia in Colombia, the massacre of students in Mexico City. I heard the bishop of Chiapas speak—he was very eloquent, and spoke a lot about peace, but I still don't speak Spanish and missed a lot.

The revolution is certainly in the air. I met lots of people doing community development work, being peace observers in poor Zapatista villages. There is even a way too hip, revolutionary-themed bar filled with young gringos . . .

On my last day in town, I went with three Spanish folks from my hostel to visit one of the Zapatista villages northeast of San Cristobal. Part way through the ride in the collectivo, going into the mountains, we met a block in the road. A few cars were lined up, and we sat in the car for a while. Down the road, there was a crowd of people. It took me a while to get the English translation that there was a man in dark green, wearing a balaclava, shot dead in the road. We all assumed the revolution was on. I only saw his boots. There were lots of native people in traditional dress (colourful dresses for women, men in black wool cloth things, some wearing broad-brimmed hats with multicoloured ribbons hanging down). It turns out that the dead man was one of two bandits who held up a car in the night. Supposedly, they only had plastic guns, but the driver being robbed had a real one. The other bandit went to hospital and this one stayed here.

So it was not Zapatista-related. Just more life and death in the South.

Bodies on the road. Holy fuck. Now he realizes that I wasn't crazy to talk about bandits.

■

I can see from my maps that Alportel is no more than 50 kilometres away over winding roads—nothing, by Canadian standards. Time is running out before I have to fly home, so I set off in the Corsa.

I drive through Benafim and Barranco do Velho, winding higher into the mountains, then down through forests of cork trees to a village that people normally speed through on their way north to Lisbon.

The place appears miraculously unchanged. A man in a brown cap squats by the side of the road with his back against a white wall, warming himself in the sun. There is the same plain white church with the same worn-out, tape-recorded bells tolling the hour. I step into the dark coolness of a store where there are open barrels of amber honey. The woman behind the counter is asleep, head on her folded arms. On the patio of Café Vitória, several old men sit as if they haven't moved for 33 years. Which might be the case.

I park the car by the highway and right away I find the overgrown footpath that goes the back way up the "mountain"—just a big hill, really. Our place was on the crest of it. Everything feels the same, even the small white wildflowers underfoot and the clarity of the air. It has a distinctive sparkle here, like Vinho Verde. I walk past barking dogs, and clucking chickens. *O tempo volta para tras.*

■

The first time I arrived here, I had taken the bus to São Brás, left my bags in a *residencia* then walked the four kilometres to Alportel, asking here and there after the tall *inglês*. They kept gesturing up the road. It was dusk by the time I left the highway and began to climb. At the top of the hill I came to a two-storey house, ochre and white, with an explosion of purple bougainvillea against one wall and grass growing up through the tiles of the patio. The dark wooden panels of the front door, with a brass knocker in the shape of a woman's hand, were narrow as a cupboard and opened down the middle. The place was elegant but slightly derelict-looking.

I had no idea what to expect. My plane mate could have a wife and family with him, if not a cult.

I knocked, then pushed open the door and there he was, like a page out of some Graham Greene novel. He was sitting in a dark leather armchair in an otherwise empty room, with a book in his lap, a cigarette between his fingers, and a glass of red wine on the floor. He was surprised to see me, but not overly.

"Amazing," he said. "I've been thinking of you the past few days, wondering if you'd come."

That night, we walked all the way back to my *residencia*, where we slept badly in the single bed, facing the painting of Jesus Christ on the wall. The next morning we brought my things back to the villa, and I moved in. His father owned the place and planned to rent it out some time. But for now it was empty.

We cooked over a brazier and lived mostly outside, where the back wall of the house jutted out into a ledge. Hours were spent just sitting on the ledge, watching the mists lift off the hills to the north. Our Portuguese neighbours were remarkably accepting of these English hippies who did nothing all day long. And it was, accidentally, domestic life, a *home*, the thing I missed but didn't realize. There wasn't even the problem of being in love, at least at first. Politics, the scene in London, my family—they all felt as far away as Jupiter. We had successfully dropped out.

Several months went by.

■

My decision to go back to Canada was as casual and careless as my arrival; it was almost Christmas, and I thought I should show up for it.

Chris walked me to the highway, where we flagged down the big smoke-windowed bus to Lisbon. I was wearing a long, three-tiered brown woollen cloak, the kind the local shepherds wore, and had packed a big bag of unshelled almonds. Although I waved from my seat on the bus I doubt he could have seen me through the tinted glass.

■

My parents lived in Burlington, near a big bridge called the Skyway, not far from the American border. On the day before Christmas, at the end of 1971, I flew to London, then New York, then took a bus north. One of Buffalo's famous snowstorms enveloped the area—the winds were strong on the arch of the Skyway. The driver agreed to drop me beside the toll booths, where my sandals sank into more than a foot of new snow: O Canada.

In my bag was a glass kerosene lamp and ceramic bowls from Portugal, presents for my parents. A cab ride took me to my parents' front door. It was early, 7:30 or so. The shoulders of my cloak were covered in snow. I was excited, breathless. My father in his bathrobe took his time answering the knock. Merry Christmas! I said, with a conscience as smooth and clean as a skating rink. His face registered surprise, anger, worry, relief, surprise, anger, like symbols rolling by in a slot machine. Either I hadn't written in weeks (a possibility) or else they hadn't received my letters. The worst part is I can't remember which it was. In any case, they weren't expecting me. They had accepted the fact that I wouldn't be home for Christmas. Now I was on their front step, in a goat-smelling cloak.

My mother appeared at the door, brought me into the house, and went about normalizing things. It was Christmas day, after all.

I sat down to proudly show my mother pictures of my travels, photos of the *inglês*, in his Indian shirt looking, I now realized as I saw him through their eyes, like a cross between a pig farmer and a dope dealer. She studied the pictures without saying a word and then went to the table, already set for 11—the whole family, minus me.

My mother added a place setting and turned my attention to the turkey on the counter, trussed and ready for the oven. Did I think five hours would be enough? We gazed at the bound bird and I tasted her dressing. No one said a thing about the fact that I had disappeared off the face of the earth or that my mother had been worried for weeks.

I couldn't see what I had done wrong. My carelessness eluded me. I was only miffed that my prodigal-daughter surprise didn't go over the way I had hoped.

But Christmas is nothing if not a set of small rituals, and these eventually salvaged the day. My mother made it clear that I was welcome, although now that I had crossed the border into her country, I would do well to put my alarming photographs away and observe the local customs instead.

I picked up a small knife and began to peel potatoes. Meanwhile, my father passed through the kitchen, cracking his knuckles in vexation and relief, working hard to forgive me.

■

When I reach the top of the hill above Alportel, the white house is still there, but it's been turned into three lavish rental units. An English couple in their sixties is staying in one; when they see me peering through the slats of the gate, they graciously invite me in. The man has a long white beard, like a hobbit, and the woman is tiny, tanned to a walnut colour, and wearing a bikini. I tour the house, where the huge blackened hearth in the kitchen is the same as I remember. So is the feel of the undulating, rosy tiles underfoot. The courtyard where the lemon and almond trees used to grow is now occupied by a swimming pool. The ledge at the back of the wall has been removed.

They are friendly and offer me a cocktail, but I say I don't want to drive the mountain roads after dark.

On my way back, I swirl into the parking lot of the Alte hotel and ding another car with my mirror. There's no damage, just a scratch on mine I will have to pay for. I log onto the computer one last time and find a brief email from Casey. He's taking a break in Puebla, he writes, and plans to meet up with two friends from Montreal who are biking their way down the Mexican coast. He'll ride with them a while, then gradually make his way back north. His hard travels seem to be behind him for now.

I buy a can of silver spray paint in town, a challenge to my Portuguese vocabulary. It covers the scratch on the mirror perfectly. Then I splurge on a phone call home to ask Brian to meet my flight. The sound of his voice steadies me. This is not a custom of ours, to pick each other up at the airport. We are very independent in our habits. In some ways, even after all these years we're still learning how to be a couple.

His Version

A MONTH OR TWO after I got back to Toronto, Casey flew home from Las Vegas with his bike in a box. His hair was wild and his eyes were very blue. Whiffs of the ocean and the desert came off him. Somewhere on the road, in a pay phone, he had applied and been accepted for a job at a summer camp in Maine, leading canoe trips. More outside. More adventure.

And he thought he might go back to university in the fall after all. Maybe change his minor to environmental studies, cut back his course load a little.

That sounds good to us, we said.

There were a few weeks left before he had to be in Maine, so he stayed with us. Sometimes he would stay out with friends 'til 3 or 4 a.m., keeping Montreal hours, then biking home. I am a light sleeper. On those nights, I fell into a certain routine.

We go to bed shortly after midnight as usual. Then, around two, my eyes pop open. I can tell by the slant of the light in the hall that his bedroom door is still open. Not home yet. Never mind! Think of all the nights he's been somewhere else, in Tucson or Tijuana or Montreal and you're not around to worry about him showing up, I chastise myself. He's in his twenties now, I remind myself, not a little boy lost in the mall; he could be driving a tank in Afghanistan. God, imagine that. (I do.)

Brian sleeps on, unperturbed, beside me. Then I think about a friend of ours, a psychotherapist with a son Casey's age still living at home; she told me that she can't help it, she stays awake 'til he gets home too. It's like we're soldiers with post-traumatic syndrome, who get triggered by harmless but familiar situations.

Three a.m. Was he wearing his helmet? I feel ridiculous, mothering away in the dark, for no good reason. Should I avail myself of the little blue crumbs of Ativan in the drawer by the bed? No, let's wait a bit. Maybe the paperman will drive by earlier than usual—his muffler is shot so I know that sound too—and I can read the *Globe*.

I don't think I have the telephone numbers of any of his Toronto friends. Alex, Tom, and Rhys. Rhys who?

Then I hear the *chunnng* of the wrought-iron fence closing and the front door unclasping. The delicate tick of the road bike being wheeled in. The fridge door opens, and closes, followed by his cautious steps on the stairs, adult and thoughtful.

The hall light goes off.

Now I can sleep.

■

Two years after our simultaneous journeys, I began to put together some notes for this book. But the chronology of events had faded, so I asked Casey to map out his itinerary for me. Also, had he thought more about why he wanted to take off and travel in the first place?

This is part of what he wrote back:

"Hitting the road was a bit of a shot in the dark. I knew I wanted a change and a new experience, but I wasn't sure what I was looking for. Part of it was a rejection of 'the establishment,' whatever that was. I've always had a chip on my shoulder about schooling and jobs and institutions. So I decided to get away and do something that wasn't tied to any of these things. The freedom was exhilarating. Every bus stop and overpass and skyline seemed unbelievably real and vivid.

"One thing I noticed is that the farther from home you get, the more your differences stick out. I was a bit of an odd character in New Mexico but I really stuck out in Guatemala. I realized I would always be having the experience of a gringo, no matter how far I travelled. I began to notice how I must have appeared to people in the middle of their own regular lives. I was a dirty, aimless white kid hundreds of miles away from his family and friends. I was going nowhere in particular, for no apparent reason. In Mexico, especially, people often couldn't understand why anyone would want to be away from their home and family.

"In Toronto, each adult person is, more or less, on their own. Not alone all the time, but when it comes down to the wire it's sort of every man for himself. You go to school to succeed, and to make a life for yourself. People work at jobs, advance their careers, buy their own things, and support their own families. If you're successful, it's your achievement. If you fail, it's your problem. The individual is the basic unit of social interaction. This puts a lot of pressure on the individual to succeed and to be an autonomous, fully functional member of society.

"In Latin America, from what I could see, the family was the basic unit of life, not the individual. People seemed to identify and understand themselves primarily according to their family, extended family, and community. It's hard to say this and not sound clichéd, but family and community seemed to mean something totally different in Mexico than it did in my world.

"I don't want to sound like a sociology textbook, so let me tell you why this is relevant to me. I was on a journey, spending time and money. I was choosing to go out into the world and find something. I was obviously doing *something*, but what the hell was it?

"First, I was getting away. I was striking out on my own and escaping my family. Why was I escaping my family? I don't know. I have and had a great family, but for some reason I felt the need to get as far away from it as possible.

"Travelling was, in one sense, eye-opening, rewarding, and mind-expanding. But in another sense, it all led nowhere. It was a treadmill. Getting away gave me lots of perspective, but it didn't leave me feeling like a well-defined individual. It was, sometimes, a little too much perspective. I was struck by how wonderful and different life could be but I didn't return with anything substantial.

"I knew when I left that I was chasing after some kind of dream. My ideas, however, were hazy. I was looking for my own version of the American dream. Not the Star-Spangled Banner version though. I was looking to discover something that spoke to the reality of America, which I saw as being sort of fallen, desperate, excessive, and glorious. I wanted to experience America first-hand, as it really was. I thought of myself as walking in the footsteps of Woody Guthrie, Bob Dylan, and Jack Kerouac—on the road."

[So, I thought, my literary suspicions are confirmed. . . .]

"In a lot of ways, I was looking for glory. (This is stereotypical of young males everywhere, but for me it was true.) When I came home, I thought I would return with stories and a broader understanding of the world. I would never have admitted that I was looking for glory, but that was surely a large part of it.

"But I found that this kind of search eventually hits the wall. I saw all kinds of people, with all kinds of lives, and all kinds of stories, but whenever I'd stop to talk with someone, the question eventually came up—'What is *your* story?' They wondered what I was doing in their world, in their town. Did I have a wife or children? Where was my family? What mattered to me, and what was I doing so far from home?

"And that always left me in a funny position, because I wasn't sure what my story was. I was part way through a history degree. I was from Toronto. My girlfriend had taken off to Hong Kong. My own world didn't make a whole lot of sense to me, so I was looking for that meaning somewhere else.

"It was like the 'Epic of Gilgamesh,' which I studied in first year, where this prince or king goes off in search of the eternal sun, or something like that. He's travelling with this half-man, half-animal guy named Enkidu. They end up finding what they're searching for then lose it in a pond. They come back home empty-handed, and that's that.

"The way I saw it, people all around me were taking rather pointless things very seriously. In university, for example, everyone took their marks and their future careers very seriously. But getting perfect marks and the perfect future didn't appeal that much to me.

"My way of rebelling was to take something pointless seriously. That's what I did with travelling. I took my aimlessness seriously.

"Although, I realize now that running off on my own into the great blue yonder was a typically North American thing to do. Individualism is a funny thing. As a frame of reference, it always makes you feel as if you're being totally original, that you're the first person ever to rebel and strike out on your own, to reject your past—when in fact, this is a terribly conventional thing to do.

"In North America, identity is not about belonging to something bigger than yourself, it's about defining yourself in contrast to everyone else. It makes sense, then, that I set out to define myself *against* the world I came from.

"But I learned that it's not so easy to be out on your own. It is exciting but it's also limited and repetitive. I wanted to be part of the big wide world, but the world actually narrows when you're on your own. It gets boring. It is also hard to have fun by yourself.

"At the end of my trip I decided that I wouldn't travel on my own in the same way again."

■

He left for the summer, before we had a chance to celebrate his twenty-first birthday. In a few weeks we got a postcard with an aerial shot of the camp, a cluster of almost invisible buildings surrounded by a swathe of forest and a large body of water. He had drawn an arrow, pointing to one red roof.

"Here I am."

The Generation Gap vs.
The Friendly Parent

I T'S HARD to remember what long-distance communication was like for families in the 1960s and '70s, and how this contributed to the gap between the values of my parents and the experimental lives of their wayward kids. My son and his friends travel the globe and never entirely leave home: we can see the set of their shoulders and monitor their haircuts on Skype; we go back and forth with them on Facebook, privy to every blip in their moods. If things go wrong, we're there to cybernetically hold their hand. Family life goes on, attenuated, but still intimate. More intimate than it used to be.

Which is good. Right?

In the late 1960s, when we went travelling it was a dramatic rupture from the family. A little death. You left home one person and might very well come back as another. The young went away to "find themselves." No one expected us to find ourselves inside the dimly lit cave of the family.

And nourishing the generation gap, staying out of touch, was easily achieved. Communication was rushed, sporadic, and superficial. Letters from home had to be sent well ahead of time, to a predetermined list of American Express offices along our route—

if we stuck with our plans. There was no expectation of sharing our experiences on the road with our families. And in many cases (smoking opium and living in caves being two examples that spring to mind) our experiences weren't of the sharing sort.

Not that drugs were to my taste; for the most part, they scared me. During university and my early twenties, I felt that my grip on my sanity, which I equated with my *self-control*, was tenuous at best, and drugs only made this worse. I was a bit afraid of losing my mind if I took acid or smoked too much dope. (This was a form of ambition, actually; one of the few adventurous options open to women in those days was to totally snap—to be Anne Sexton or Sylvia Plath, brilliant and broken.)

I became adept at contact highs, however.

Communication with my family consisted of letters scribbled on thin blue sheets of airmail stationery. The post office sold these with the stamps already on; you filled one side with writing, then folded it into an envelope that slowly made its way, with its already stale news, to my parents, who anxiously awaited the arrival of the postman every morning, in case he brought news of my survival in unimaginable foreign lands.

In 1969, my family accepted the notion of a post-grad European trek, preferably with a Eurail Pass in hand. It counted as continuing education; we were "broadening" ourselves. But for them travel signified marble statues and historical ruins, not hitchhiking in strange cars and smoking dope in Amsterdam cafés.

That winter I was in Europe with my boyfriend, a tall poetry-writing lad from another nice family who would clearly protect me from bad men. In those days the hippie trail either led east from London to India, south to Ibiza off the coast of Spain or to Greece and the caves of Matala, which a feature in *Life* magazine had already made semi-famous. (Joni Mitchell arrived a month or two after we left and met the red-haired chef who inspired the song "Carey." Several years later the bubonic plague broke out, and the idyll was over.)

After moving into a spacious cave with a view of the sea, I updated my family on our itinerary.

"The three of us are living in a small fishing village on the southern coast of Crete," I wrote, having invented a chaperone-ish third party to offset the unavoidably domestic overtones of living as a couple in a cave. "This is a Greek archeological site," I added (educational). "The cliffs have rows of man-made caves that date back to the Neolithic period, where travellers can stay for free" (frugality). "We are staying in one of the larger caves. It's very nice and has a door" (a tarpaulin). "The ocean is clean and perfect for swimming. The local fishermen sell fresh fish on the beach" (nutrition). "We're getting a tan and enjoying a rest after being on the road all winter." 55

Ah, the daughterly wiles of the young suburban hippie.

I doubt they imagined me hallucinating Jesus Christ on cough syrup (one of the preferred drugs at Matala was the cough medicine Romilar, a mix of speed and codeine). Although, I shouldn't underestimate my mother's lurid imagination about the bad things that might happen to me. She once warned me about a bacterial infection that you could catch from playing the bagpipes (not my instrument). And of course I wasn't writing long anguished emails to them about my relationship, or my own Premarin-fuelled nuttiness.

My mother worked hard to accept my adventures, having always been a freethinker and a science-minded rationalist. This was her brand of feminism, I think—a crisp lack of sentiment. Long before it became fashionable, her mantra was "it's all chemistry" regarding addiction, dereliction, and sex offenders; for her it was all about the brain, and science has since caught up with her. Among other things, genes and chemistry explained homosexuality, which she accepted decades before the era of Gay Pride. After earning her degree in math and home ec (a combination that describes her well) she worked as a switchboard operator in Saskatoon. But in those early Depression days, couples were only allowed to hold down one job per household, and so when she married she had to stop working.

I just assumed the gap between my mother's life and mine was unbridgeable. She had met my father when they were 13 and 14, and by their mid-twenties they had married and had their first child. She dated a few others along the way and had the odd crush, she let me know, on other men, including her sister's boyfriend. He was a dashing fighter pilot—are there any other kind?—named Ernie McNab, who once flew low over the university campus in his plane and waggled his wing tips at them.

But the concept of sleeping with different guys just because you were attracted to them was new to her, although it made sense, she thought, to try them out before you settle for one. As she used to mildly, somewhat admiringly muse, as I pursued the single life into my thirties, "Yes, you've had a lot of boyfriends."

She never criticized me for not marrying (I recanted at the age of 50). But she worried that I would get hurt. Which, of course, I did. It became a bit of a pattern, in fact. I had talked myself out of wanting anything resembling "commitment," but that turned out to eliminate too much.

Her reply to my letter describing our cave life was tactful and carefully upbeat. She caught me up on the family news—all good, in the style of the Christmas form letter, in which no doubt or heartache intrudes. Then she gave me a recipe for non-rising Irish soda bread, easily cooked in an iron frying pan on an open fire.

"Enjoy!" she gallantly signed off.

◼

Earlier, while we were hitchhiking through Europe, she sent me letters with newspaper clippings about date-rape drugs. She warned me never to sit beside a stranger in a bar, who could jab a hypodermic needle into my thigh and cart me off as a sex slave.

Honestly, I thought, what was her problem?

The thing is, technically, she was right. Girls do fall into the hands of bad men. Women are sold as sex slaves. Date-rape drugs remain popular and effective. But at the time, I saw it as just another example of my mother's xenophobic, unhip fears about "other people" (usually "swarthy").

My letters home from Europe that year were superficial, chipper, and full of evasion: the Goya paintings in the Prado were so much more impressive in person; there are a million stray cats in the Coliseum; the hostel in Thessalonika has this neat rooftop café; and so on. "Greg got a nail in his heel from his old boots—I keep telling him to get new ones," I would report with wifely exasperation. "Greg is writing a very detailed journal—thank goodness one of us is keeping track!"

I do not tell my mother about the man with the knife in the Marrakesh hostel. I don't tell my father that while hitchhiking to Bari, in Italy, we were picked up by a convicted rapist who kept us hostage for hours, until the police came to our rescue. And I don't mention that my gentle poet boyfriend slept with the girl in the cave next door. I went through my betrayals and depressions by myself, without my family—or, for that matter, the comfort of girlfriends. The sexual revolution predated the women's movement by a few ragged years.

Meanwhile, we were taking heavy-duty drugs: birth control pills that delivered veterinary levels of hormones and left us vulnerable to disease; acid: mushrooms and assorted mind-benders that other cultures surround with protective rituals and wise mentors. We put evil-looking IUDs like the Dalkon Shield into our wombs, devices that left thousands of women infertile. The notion of "free love," in short, was a crock. But we went along with it. It was our equivalent of new software.

■

My parents hadn't travelled widely, and they feared the worst about European capitals. They imagined streets riddled with thieves, derelicts, and drug addicts—and, as it happened, when they did make it overseas that is exactly what they managed to attract, wherever they went.

On their first flight to London, the man sitting in the seat across the aisle from my mother died of a heart attack or a stroke. The flight was completely booked; dragging a body up the aisles was not an option, so the attendants had to drape a sheet over the poor man until they landed at Heathrow. In relating this story, my mother was quite sanguine and worldly, as if dead bodies were simply one of the little glitches one encountered on transcontinental flights. I was aghast. They were stepping into what they thought of as "my world," and it was turning out to be as lurid as they had imagined.

I accompanied my parents on one of their first experiences riding the Underground in London. Burlington does not have a subway. Saskatoon did not have a subway. I've always looked upon urban public transit as a heartwarming democratic vision, where the citizens of a big city peaceably huddle together. I was eager to show off the splendour of the labyrinthine London Tube to my parents; my engineer father in particular, I thought, would be impressed by this clever inverted system of bridges.

We were in the Underground, on our way to the Tower of London. My parents sat side by side, smiling in their encouraging fashion at the commuters around them, who either ignored them or gave faint, stiff smiles in return. Across the aisle from us was a tall, painfully thin man, hanging onto the overhead strap. He seemed boneless and loose as he swayed like a weed in a stream with each lurch of the subway car. It was my mother who first noticed the hypodermic needle dangling from one bicep. Then I saw it, just as his head lolled back.

"Oh dear, how can he stand up," she said, reasonably enough. In all my wanderings through all the wrong parts of foreign cities, in the back lanes of Tangiers or Istanbul, I had never encountered a junkie who didn't bother to take the needle out of his arm.

Miraculously, the man continued to hang from his strap, head pendulum-ing, chin bouncing off his chest, pants inching down his ass. Other passengers stared straight ahead. My father gave me an "Oh well!" sort of thumbs-up look, which made me feel better. We hustled out of the car and rode the escalators up, up into the daylight without discussing the incident.

A day or two later, on their way to Hampstead Heath, my parents encountered a homeless woman begging. Instead of putting coins in her hand and moving on, they sat down on the curb and got in a conversation with her.

"Her husband left and took all her savings with him—boy, she sure knows how to pick 'em," said my father, relating their street adventure with relish. They gave her a little money and wished her well before they went on their way. I worried that they might have invited her to move to Canada and into their spare room (my room). My parents in their forties were innocents abroad—more innocent, I realized, than I was at 21.

In 1969 and 1970, there were many things I couldn't share with my parents, despite their loving support and my respect for them: drugs, for instance. The first time Greg met my family, he was on acid. "What a big smile Greg has," my mother later remarked, approvingly. And sex, of course. Apart from giving me a book called *The Wonderful Story of You* and telling me to drink cranberry juice to prevent cystitis, my mother and I never discussed sex or contraception. There may have been a few forced jokes while watching a movie. "Well, I hope that she's on the pill, or she's in for trouble," she might say in the course of *Gidget Goes Hawaiian*.

We never talked about writing either, a perilous pursuit in their eyes. In my parents' eyes, creativity was for hobbies. They wanted me to be a schoolteacher or a secretary, en route to marriage and motherhood. "You'll always have your typing" was what my mother said when she bought me my first typing book, in Grade 8.

And, indeed, I do.

■

The rule of the generation gap was for both sides to put on a good face—at least, in middle-class WASP families this was the case. There were other households where fighting, cursing, and door-slamming went on, but not in mine. As a result, they didn't know what I went through, as I grappled with sex, love, and my sanity; and I didn't hear about their struggles either.

How close should families be? I am still confused about that.

■

A big contributing factor to the new intimacy in families is the utterly different ratio of parents to children in this generation. The old balance of two parents vs. a bunch of siblings has become rare in North America (unless you're on reality TV). Single children, or two at most, are the norm.

Only children grow up with enormous pressures upon them to fulfill the family destiny. Compounding the situation, the number of single parents living with only children has risen since my upbringing. It's easy for the single parent to fall into a quasi-marital relationship with their school-age kids, bringing them along to adult occasions and absorbing them into the culture of the parents. The thing is, kids are often better company than the departed spouses. And sometimes the power struggles aren't as daunting as they are in adult relationships, because in the end they are the parent, in charge of the child. There is no anxiety about the relationship ending because it will never end; they will always be the mother, or the father. The role is permanent, a tattoo—unlike other kinds of love, alas.

I worry that these only children, cast in the role of mini-wives and mini-husbands, will grow up with a deep sense of being indispensable to their parent.

I'm not peering over the fence here, by the way. There was a degree of singleness involved in my own early motherhood, when Brian was freelancing and often out of town on assignments. The daily stuff of raising Casey belonged largely to me. So I was grateful for my son's company. Even at four (especially at four, actually). He liked to talk, he was reflective and funny—I deeply enjoyed our relationship. But I hope I didn't *count* on his company.

I'm sure he has felt the weight of being an only child and the weight of our love for him, our desire to solve his problems and see him happy. I wish he had siblings. He's had to grow a bit of armour in order not to respond too quickly to other people's expectations. Or to ours.

■

In my family, I have a brother seven years older and a sister seven years younger. Twenty-one years of diapers. And while I was drifting around Europe, as it turned out, my parents were coping with serious family issues. Teenage rebellions, shaky first marriages, health crises—it was all going on back home, and my parents had to perform some search-and-rescue missions. It must have been mystifying for them: the family they had so carefully engineered, their great life achievement, seemed to be buckling under various stresses. Meanwhile, their middle daughter, while not yet in rehab, was gadding about the world wasting her education and talents.

When my well-behaved little sister ran off to Quebec City at the age of 16 my father phoned me, upset. They had just read her note, saying she'd be back in a few days and not to worry.

"Maybe there's still time to intercept her at the airport," he said. Of course I thought they should "trust her" and let her go.

"It's your lifestyle that's partly to blame for this," my father said in a rare angry outburst.

■

Now the pendulum has swung to the other side, from the Generation Gap to the Fused Family. We share so much with our children that carving out our autonomy, and letting our kids pursue theirs, has become another something we must work at. Note to self: back off. I await the new manuals on "Learning to Un-Mother."

The generation gap made it easier for us to stay selfish, confused, and adrift in the embrace of youth culture, which helped us believe that our world was more interesting than any other world. Of course, everyone in their early twenties enters a self-involved orbit to a greater or lesser extent. It's the decade when you give birth to your adult self, and an inward focus is part of that. But my lack of trust in my parents' ability to handle my *real* life only increased the emotional gap between us. We loved each other and were unusually tolerant of our different paths. Classic post-war liberal optimists, the bunch of us. But I think we settled for too much distance.

Landscaping
the Family

WHEN WE MOVED into our current house, we inherited a number of extravagant touches from the concert-pianist, flute-playing, interior-designing woman who lived here before us. The bedroom was painted a glossy eggplant black with gold trim. The bed not only had a canopy but flaming electric torches.

"That's a lot to live up to," Brian remarked.

The little room that would become my office had nothing in it but a harpsichord and a dressmaker's form wearing a French Empire gown, like a headless Marie Antoinette. The first floor featured an impressive copy of a painting by the 18th-century French painter Fragonard, executed right on the wall. For an extra $20,000, we could keep it. (Think of the resale potential: "Three bdrm semi, hdwd flrs, blt-in Fragonard. . . .") But we declined. The owner, who wore a bustier and drove a red pickup truck, peeled it off the wall, and took it with her.

The house was small but theatrical—perfect for family dramas. The kitchen had a working wood stove and doors that opened onto a garden, where the owner had set out a white wrought-iron table for two, with linen napkins and wine glasses. Not my usual workday lunch . . . but it could be, if we bought her house.

The garden was a lush, feminine affair with pink roses, lilac trees, and a minuscule pond. More of a basin. But with a water feature, I thought, my life could really turn around. A flagstone path also led through the garden to a gate that opened onto the lane. The escape route.

The house is a narrow, fine-boned Victorian, perfect for one. Casey was 17 when we moved, with bicycles, amplifiers, and skateboards. Brian is over six feet tall; whenever he walks down the main hall the floors bounce slightly, like a suspension bridge. He looks like a sailor on a small craft making his way to the forward deck. The ceilings are high, and the doorbell is 110 years old. Casey's friends were just across the bridge, in our old neighbourhood, so he was okay with the move.

But Brian wasn't convinced.

"We're already living in a three-bedroom semi," he pointed out, "why move to another one?" By then I had looked at 57 properties, from crumbling rectories in Port Hope to time-warp cottages in Mimico. This eccentric house, on a lilac-laden street, was the one for us, I knew. So when Brian continued to come up with more sensible reasons not to buy it, I didn't argue. I simply went to bed. It wasn't a calculated sulk; I was just giving up on my pond-worthy future.

Several days passed.

"Well, I'll take another look at it," Brian said.

We made an offer, and the deal was done. The middle bedroom, we rationalized, would soon become an office for one of us when Casey left for college the following year. This, of course, has not happened, because that was his room when he came home from school for visits. We got used to the close quarters, though. We live in a Victorian sailboat, snug and trim.

I had visions for the pond and bought a small motorized pump. I wanted to hear gentle plashing whenever I sat out at the wrought-iron table in a French way. I plugged the pump into a long extension cord that snaked through the garden, turned it on, admired the turbulence, and then went to bed.

But the street is close to a ravine and its wildlife. I had already noticed the evidence of raccoon slumber parties—flattened crop circles—in the peony beds. The next morning, the pond was silent. The raccoons, offended by strange pulsings in their ensuite, had hauled the pump out of the pond and hidden it in the bushes nearby.

I reinstalled it and turned it back on. Plashing restored, I ate a tomato sandwich at the patio table, with a cloth napkin on my lap.

Next morning, more silence. This time the raccoons had stashed the motor farther back in the bushes. It was time to get industrial. I sank a device the size of a shoebox into the pond and stepped back from the great gush of water that now rocketed out of the tiny basin. The raccoons were about to be hosed down by the riot police.

That evening, I watched five of them plumply scuttle along the top of our fence. They gave a wide berth to the pond, churning like a hydroelectric generator. In the lane, the garbage was lashed down with bungee cords. I slept soundly that night.

When I came down the next morning, I made French-press coffee and took the paper outside to my table.

Silence.

This time the raccoons had dragged the pump, still running, into the weeds behind the lilac tree. Now the motor had burned out. Another $280 down the drain.

Finally, I ceded the pond to the raccoons, but this episode led to an escalating neglect of the whole backyard. I no longer flossed the flagstones or staked the clematis. Every once in a while, I would go on a defoliating rampage, pulling up the spearmint that had overtaken one side, and whacking back the roses, tiny starved blossoms at the end of great pole-vaulting shoots. Then that stopped too.

Whenever I feel my environment getting out of control, I decide I have "more important things" to do—writing books, ordering bathing suits online, etc. My field of vision begins to iris in until I only see what I need to. I can find the scissors in the kitchen drawer, but I don't notice the 22 wine corks. I see the last bit of goat cheese hiding in the refrigerator, but not the furry chutney at the front.

This carelessness is something that our son doesn't share, despite his own deliberate spheres of chaos. He has always been quietly disappointed by the amount of rot that goes on at the back our refrigerator, with its tubs of boutique olives languishing in their brine. I think our ability to live with a certain amount of entropy—to *not take care of things*—strikes him as a moral failing, and he may have a point. We waste a lot of food, because leftovers aren't . . . fresh.

Brian especially fetishizes freshness, which I suspect is a remnant from his English background, where you go round to the shops every day, chat with the shopkeepers, and leave with some nice pink chops. Fish must be glistening and bright-eyed, barely off life support. His standards for raspberries are also high; at the first little wisp of mould, he's out the door to buy fresher, dewier, ones. (There is a sexual metaphor here that I'm not going to pursue.)

Our domestic blind spots are ironic given that we're journalists, paid to notice details. We can catch the smallest continuity glitch in a movie while overlooking the broken security light above the barbecue, the one that has been swinging open since we moved in.

This would have appalled my engineer father. When I was growing up, we had a Kenmore dryer that ran for 30 years. Twenty years in, it began to make a funny noise, but "if you just put a drop of oil in the motor before you use it, it works perfectly," he would say. We got another decade of use out of it before the lint in the lint catcher finally caught fire and filled the basement with smoke.

Still. It was the thought that counted: the caretaking.

Now, whenever our son is due for a visit home, I cast a critical eye on the garden and inside the fridge. I want not to disappoint him. If he catches me with greasy black parsley in the crisper, I will feel derelict. It's not that he's a prim environmental nag; what I think he means is, *pay attention*. See what's really there in front of you, not just what you want to see. This applies to our relationship with him, too.

We blame our not-seeing on our deadlines and tunnel vision (the writer's one-size-fits-all excuse). It's also our leftover 1960s notion that we have better things to do than to Scotchgard the sofa or tend to worldly things.

On the other hand, at 23 Casey has no interest in acquiring things; his belongings can be stored in several milk crates, three guitar cases, and a backpack. He has more amplifiers than furniture. He's frugal, but frugality can also be a sort of inverted materialism, one that confers too much negative power to "stuff." For a long time, he considered shampoo a consumerist ruse and he wasn't going to fall for it. Hand soap would do nicely, even if his hair had the sheen of someone with an immune disease. That phase ended, but new clothes are still tricky. Last Christmas, I bought him what I thought was a foolproof non-trendy T-shirt with no labels. It did have stripes, but they were vintage stripes.

"No more buying me clothes," he said gently but firmly, folding it up and putting it back in the box.

■

Casey has always gone his own way, without taking us on as adversaries. At the same time, the three of us also share a lot, including music. We can all listen to Neil Young and Sam Cooke and Louis Armstrong. Sometimes on holiday we'll play music together (Brian on congas, me on idiot-savant violin, and Casey on guitar). We've never been "the enemy" to him, and he has been honest with us about whatever he's going through. I assumed that this lack of open conflict in our family was a good thing.

What I had forgotten, of course, was my own long drift away from my own family—something that "lack of conflict" also bred.

Children growing up are sooner or later going to draw the line between their lives and their parents' lives. And it has to be a little painful; it has to feel like a genuine rupture. Most of the time, this happens in adolescence, with the usual showdowns. But the twenties are a good time to do it too.

■

One summer I was out west on a month-long assignment, so Casey ended up spending that time cohabiting with his father and sharing household duties. When Brian flew out for a visit, Casey was left with the job of closing up the house.

"Dad, just to let you know," he emailed Brian, "fridge rot does not take care of itself."

I came back home briefly, before packing up to go to the cottage. I stepped out into the yard, where the grapevines at the back of the garden were running amok and about to strangle the lilac tree. Casey was in the kitchen, eating breakfast. He would join us later, for a few days' holiday.

"Casey," I said, "can you take care of the grapevines at the back of the yard? Just take out whatever's crowding out the good stuff."

But later that week, he arrived at the cottage with the grim air of being on a mission. He said he'd "been thinking" and that he "needed to talk," with Brian in particular. Uh-oh, I thought. Time to peel a quart of peaches and turn the radio on.

The two of them went down to the dock, where Casey sat his father down for a long conversation about their differences—and, more critically, their similarities. He was having trouble, he said, because he could see just how much he shared with us, but there were some ways in which he didn't *want* to be like us. And instead

68

of the usual slow, alienated slide away from parents, he wanted to deal with our differences. Have it out. We were all good at getting along, he agreed, but we were totally lame at conflict.

Every once in a while I'd look out the window and see Brian with his head down, solemnly nodding, as Casey leaned forward and spoke. Later, in the middle of the night, I tried to reassure Brian.

"This happens when boys grow up," I said, whispering so as not to wake up Casey. "You're the father, and he needs to smite you. He has smote you, or whatever the past tense is, with his sword. He's saying that you no longer set the agenda."

One of the things that is good about being at the lake is the utter darkness, on moonless nights. We lay there in the silence.

"Try not to take it personally," I said.

69

■

So, not a relaxing week at the cottage. I think Casey wanted us to break out of that WASPy way of never fighting or feeling the connection that comes with honest, open clashes. He was tired of pretending that we agreed about everything just because we liked some of the same tunes.

Herbert Marcuse, a philosopher and political theorist popular back in the 1960s, had a term for this, a phrase I grabbed onto in my own seething, conflict-free youth: repressive tolerance. When all is permitted, where are the edges of things, the points of contact?

We had also given him the impression, growing up, that whatever he did or wanted in life was just fine with us. Of course, this wasn't strictly true, and he knew it: there were unspoken expectations of him that arose from our undefined but fairly rigid set of values. Self-expression and creativity, for instance, over success in business. (Our mistake!) Friendship and community over individualism and the rat race. We didn't talk about these assumptions but we didn't have to; he grew up marinated in them.

I thought I didn't have a master plan in mind for him. But it meant more to me than I realized that he finish his university degree, even though I had had no problem fleeing academia the minute I graduated. And yes, I promoted medical school too (my phantom career). I also kept encouraging him to put his musical talents out there. For years he had written and recorded a lot of songs that I never tired of listening to, even with my non-maternal ears. He would point out (as many parents might) that the world is not undersupplied with talented songwriters.

"But you *like* performing," I would respond.

Since when do mothers try to persuade their sons to join rock bands?

Brian didn't push him. He knew he would find his own way with his music. But he too put a higher value on "art" than "a career in public health." This was the result of our having grown up in a culture where jobs were plentiful and money was not a burning issue.

But in the new world, money was most definitely an issue. Casey understood this more than we did.

In his twenty-fourth summer, Casey was trying to draw that line between us and him. This was normal, it's how growing up works. But it gave me pause. Maybe pretending to be a happy little family is always an elaborate game of self-deception to get us all through.

Casey went down to Montreal and we stayed on at the cottage, where thoughts of the garden back home kept intruding. Why did I think a "natural" garden was a good thing, better than uptight landscaping? Wasn't it better to be bossy with the life-choking weeds, to admit that you're in charge and that gardens need some discipline?

How much bare soil is required for healthy growth? How much to rip out, how much to leave alone? Pruning is supposed to be healthy for plants, I knew that much, and cutting things back helps things grow, in the end.

As parents, I thought, maybe we should have weeded more. Not because our son needed more discipline, but because then our roles would have been more distinct.

■

In mid-August, a bit subdued by our time at the cottage, we came back to Toronto and the house that Casey had closed up before he left the city.

We unpacked the car and aired out the house. Opened the doors to the garden. I braced myself for the usual late-summer accumulation of neglect: the overgrown yard, the piled-up bills, our city life to reclaim. And . . . for what? What was the whole point of home, again?

I walked in and saw my bike panniers tucked away in the hall. Had he remembered to leave my bike key? Yes, there it was in the lock. I passed through the well-ordered house. Were the orchids dead? No, they were thriving, and had sent out new tendrils. The fridge was clean and empty. I stepped into the yard, where the red hibiscus had produced an almost grotesquely huge blossom.

But the most striking change was that Casey had cleaned up the full width and length of the flagstones that led to the back of the yard. He had ripped up all the weeds, pried the grass out from between the stones, cut away the invading grapevines, breached the undergrowth that had caused us to give up on the entrance to the laneway.

It was such a welcoming sight. He had restored order to the garden not by stuffing it with exotic shrubs or installing "water features," but by uncovering the structural elements that had been there all the time.

Now the plants could breathe. All we had to do was to maintain the path he had cleared for us.

That's That

I was bent over in Uttanasana when I saw Brian thread
through the class toward me. My yoga partner, a tall guy with
stork legs, was pushing down on my sacrum. The teacher
said, "Come up slowly, Marni."

Brian had a neutral but bright-eyed expression and a slightly
fixed smile. A strange vision in the middle of yoga class. I followed
him outside into the hall.

"What's wrong?" I said, with thoughts of Casey first.

"It's Clyde," Brian said, holding me.

"He's in the hospital?"

"No," he said in a wondering voice, "he's dead." He put his arms
around me.

"I'm not surprised, I'm not surprised," I cried. "I spoke to my
mother on the phone today and I could tell she was worried about
him."

But of course, I was shocked to the core. Apart from the stomach problems he had been having for the past few weeks, my 94-year-old father was rarely ill. I never saw him in bed during the
day. Trust him to make such a whistle-clean exit.

Brian and I drove straight to Burlington without saying much.

A shawl of calm descended on me; I felt clear and cool. Everyone else in the family was already on the scene when we arrived. My sister-in-law Kathy opened the door, and we cried together. Jori was dry-eyed, but her mouth was twisted down. Bruce was sitting on the couch in the den looking flushed.

"Where is she?" my mother said, moving through the halls. She tottered toward me with an almost ironic "Wouldn't you know death would come along?" expression on her face. She looked short and white. I said, "Oh Mom," and put my hands on her face. Then I held her. She appeared chagrined and rueful.

Jori's husband, Wayne, had the flu and had gone home rather than risk passing it on to my mother. Casey was up north in Quebec, working for the owners of our cottage. I decided the call could wait 'til tomorrow. Let him have one happy day in the woods.

Everyone was in the den, drinking sherry. Brian opened a bottle of red wine and brought me a glass, a big one.

"So tell me the gory details," I said.

"Well, we had a really good day," my mother began. "He'd been having pain for days before, but this afternoon he told the doctor that he was feeling a little better. Then he said he wanted meat and potatoes for dinner—'no more tinned salmon.' We went out in the car, bought some groceries, and on our way back he decided to pay a bill at Sears. He went in alone. I thought, I ought to go in with him, but he said no, stay in the car. When we got back home I said, 'Oh let's have a drink.'"

He hadn't been drinking because of the medication he was on, she explained, but he'd been off the drug for a week.

"So we both had a weak gin and tonic. I said, 'Why don't you just stretch out on the couch while I get dinner?' because he was looking so tired, and I went into the kitchen to get it ready. He was in the bathroom when I heard some sort of noise and went in. He had fallen and was trying to pull himself up. . . ."

My mother went on to describe how she helped him lie down and went to fetch a pillow to put under his head. His eyes grew wide as they looked at one another, and she knew that he knew that this was it. She called my brother, who phoned 911.

"When we arrived, the paramedics were just pulling out in the ambulance," said Bruce. "Slowly, with the lights off."

The calm of shock prevailed. My mother was quite present, which I marvelled at. Here we were, sitting around as if waiting for dips and dinner, in the lee of our father's death.

Jori and I stayed overnight with my mother, who lent me the white summer nightgown I had given her years before. I hadn't brought a change of clothes or even a toothbrush. When it was time to go to bed, I used the downstairs bathroom he had died in, aggressively. Everything had a different aspect now—the little scissors he used to trim his moustache, his eye drops, his black comb and square brush. Jori stayed in Bruce's old room, while I slept next door to her, beside my parents' bedroom.

When she was settled in bed, my mother put her headphones on as usual to listen to Art Bell. Whenever she couldn't sleep, which was often, she listened to his all-night call-in program, where supernatural theories were floated and people phoned in to describe their abduction by aliens. It distracted her through the long night. I kept surfacing from sleep to hear the leakage of radio voices from her room as she patiently lay there. I woke at six and thought, "Daddy." I remembered being a little girl, going fishing with him down along the lakeshore. I felt him swarming through the house, anxious about us.

In the morning my mother was up first, and wearing the big grey bathrobe that her grandson had brought back from Asia for her. "It's so warm, I wear it all the time," she said conversationally. Jori was having a shower, so the two of us sat together on the broadloomed steps in the hall, waiting for her to come out.

"It's just like old times," Jori laughed when she saw us. We were all without makeup and looking utterly haggard. As usual, my mother got out the breakfast cereals and the bowl of unshelled nuts. Every morning she and my father had cereal with raisins, banana, and freshly cracked walnuts and almonds on top. This we had and sat down with tea.

Mornings are not good for my mother at the best of times. Her hands shake and she is at low ebb. We talked about who to phone and what to do. Jori knew all their friends, the ones still alive at least, and she would call them. My sister was the haircutter for most of them. I would put the death notice in the local paper. I was the writer.

My mother got dressed and, with hands that trembled more than usual, sat trying to read the *Globe*. I composed a death notice to my mother's strict, Quakerish requirements. No flourishes allowed. Then the curiously mundane details of dealing with the body of someone who has died carried us along from one hour to the next.

■

The director of Just Cremation was vacuuming when I happened by. It wouldn't do to have dusty surfaces in this line of work. The shop was a small storefront affair, handily across from the Egertson Funeral Home, where my father now reposed.

"I'll be right with you," the director said. He had large, liquid brown eyes. I sat down in one of two winged Victorian armchairs that faced his gilt-edged desk and took one of his business cards. *Armand Alazzi*. A Lebanese or Armenian name, unusual for Burlington, where I had grown up without encountering a single dark-skinned person. The director had a full brush-like moustache and smooth, thick, springy hair. He smiled apologetically as he moved the mouth of the vacuum back and forth over the broadloom, and we shared its high-pitched, indignant noise.

My mother for years had instructed us that there was to be no funeral service, and no fuss was to be made of their deaths. Always in the plural; having done everything together for 68 years my mother and father assumed they would die together too. It would be like the two of them finding a parking spot at the mall—she was the spotter, he was the driver. Whenever I came home to visit, my father would open the bottom drawer of his mahogany pull-down desk to point to "the arrangements," as he always called them.

"You only need to make one phone call. Call Egertson's, and they'll take care of everything." He knew that tidy business arrangements and planning for the future were not our forte.

"I don't want any strangers gawking at me," my mother would always add at that point. She had a horror of funerals with an open casket, and of trays of crustless sandwiches passed among the curious. She had already embarked on a course of electrolysis because, as she put it, "I don't want to have a stroke and be lying in some hospital bed with hairs sprouting out of my face." Being seen dead was a concern.

"Just send us up the chimney and come home and have a glass of sherry," she would say with a kind of gay irritability whenever we tried to protest. But now that some of my friends were being picked off by cancer, I began to find the conventions of funerals reassuring. Someone thought to make sandwiches, another friend could be counted on to say the wrong thing, so-and-so would get drunk and stay too long—it all kept you clasped in the present. The mundanity of funerals said that life with its pots of tea and mixed motives would go on.

But burning a person, it turned out, was not as simple as a phone call. There were laws about human remains, and the question of scattering, or interment, and then the business of what to put the ashes in, and who in the family would keep them. As murderers and widows come to learn, it takes surprising enterprise and a certain amount of work to truly rid yourself of the body.

I think my mother was in shock. The fact that my father would leave her side forever and ever, just as a hot dinner was about to be served, was not something she could quickly grasp. So instead of weeping and falling apart, she applied herself to this practical problem—the recipe, as it were, for her husband's ashes. As with a casserole, first came the matter of choosing the appropriate dish.

After an urn-tour of the house, we settled on a rather eccentric swirly blue ceramic vase, something my mother had made. My sister had fashioned a lid for it by gluing together several plywood discs that I had bought at the craft store. An ad hoc sort of urn. I delivered the vessel to Just Cremation, and my mother and I retired to the den with large glasses of sherry. There would be no service, just the family, and a brief "visitation."

78

"Well," my mother said, "that's that."

But that wasn't that at all.

A Serious
Little Mountain

T HE DAY AFTER my father died, I called Casey in Quebec
to give him the news. During that first night it comforted
me to know that he was up in the woods with his surrogate
family, engaged in the safest, most bucolic activity imaginable—
making maple syrup.

It reminded me of the phone calls from Brian's mother, who at
91 is frail but still living in her own home.

"So Marni's fine and Casey's fine?" Yes, Brian tells her.

"So everyone's okay." The mantra we need to repeat.

Another consolation was that my father had died without ever
being aware of the dangerous episodes in my life. I hadn't told him
about that little sea plane ride where I watched the co-pilot poke a
broom through a hole in the cabin to get the landing wheels un-
stuck. Or how our South American bike ride ended in the Atacama
Desert of northern Peru, with chest pains and the world's longest
taxi ride to Lima.

With Casey, of course, it was the opposite—we knew all too
well what he was up to. Or so we thought. A few weeks earlier, after
the school term had ended, Casey had told us that he was heading

out to the Maritimes on a camping trip with his girlfriend Julia. They were going to climb Gros Morne mountain in Newfoundland. An easy day trip in good weather, according to the website. They planned to hitchhike there, but this was eastern Canada not Nevada. I paid scant attention.

However, things did not go as planned. I was spared the details until sometime later, when Casey decided to write an account of their trek up Gros Morne. Here is part of it:

"After what seemed like a few hours of climbing we came to a high plateau, with a wooden platform. I looked out onto the plain and saw grass, bushes, and wind-blown trees. Rising up ahead of us stood the peak of Gros Morne. On the platform was a sign:

Gros Morne, at 803 meters above sea-level, is the second highest mountain in Newfoundland. Up above the tree-line, we are now in an exposed environment resembling the Arctic tundra. This barren land is home to wildlife such as Rock Ptarmigans, Arctic Hares and Woodland Caribou. The vegetation is fragile and the soil is prone to wind erosion. The trail to the summit will take you up a steep boulder gully. You will pass through several distinct ecological zones, each a different habitat for plants and animals.

"The plaque gave a number of advisories. 'Be prepared for rapid changes in temperature, lack of water, high wind and blistering sun.'

"There was also something along the lines of 'Please stay on the trail at all times. The vegetation is old and fragile. The trail is steep and the gully can be dangerous to descend as there is a risk of dislodging boulders onto climbers below.'

"Also, most importantly, 'The mountain is closed until the beginning of July.' We were there in April, with patches of snow still on the ground.

"For some reason, this didn't faze us. I saw it as just another piece of paperwork, like one of those 'Do you accept the following terms' contracts required to do most things. From where we stood, the peak appeared to be quite close. It was grey in colour and round in shape—almost friendly-looking.

"I decided that these warnings were intended for other less wilderness-savvy individuals—people with fanny packs and carbon fibre walking sticks. Gros Morne was a day hike. Besides, we still had a good three or four hours of sunlight left, and there wasn't a cloud in the sky.

"As we stood in front of the sign, I remember feeling a spark of hesitation. It was a subtle but familiar sensation. It begins with a potentially risky situation and a decision to be made. Is the lake too windy to paddle across? Is this set of rapids too big to run safely? On day 15, is it wise to eat the pre-cooked Mexican Beef with a little hole in the package?

"From the platform we could see the trail winding through the alpine field above us, past a few small lakes and up to the base of the peak. From there, a series of cairns pointed to a rock gully that appeared to be the most direct route up—except that the middle of the gully was filled with snow. It was a case of either slogging through the snow or climbing up the bare but rocky edges of the gully.

"I considered the challenges of walking on jagged rocks blanketed by snow, in sneakers. Prime ankle-spraining territory. I had visions of avalanches, the kind that begin as a tiny clump of displaced snow.

"All of a sudden, we were no longer on a nature walk; we were two people on a mountain. Only half an hour had passed and we were in a totally different environment. The sun was brighter. The air felt dryer. We were leaving the earth behind and entering the realm of the sky.

"As we climbed, we encountered bigger rocks, in the breadbox-to-blue-box size range. The grade became steeper, and soon we had to use our hands. At first it was fun and easy, like climbing a tree. From time to time a clump of rocks shifted under my weight, but for the most part things seemed stable.

"We were now officially high up. From this perspective, the slope below us looked much steeper, and the trail we had just taken through the fields looked like a piece of string connecting the lakes. The sight gave me another shock of doubt.

"Things were getting a little more serious, a little more technical. Going up, the way became narrower, and it wasn't clear how far we would have to climb. Going down, the footing was unstable. Either way was bad.

"I tested the sliding effect again with a careful step. The rocks gave way under my foot, and I watched them tumble down, down, down. This is how landslides are made, I thought. I was afraid. Someone had just turned up the voltage knob in my brain.

"We turned and climbed on in silence, with slow and careful steps. I took account of our situation. As far as I could tell, we were the only people on this mountain. And to make it worse, nobody knew we were up here. Nobody was expecting us home for dinner.

"I imagined the newspaper headlines: 'Two Hitchhikers Found Stranded on Gros Morne.' Or worse: 'Tourists Ignore Posted Warnings and Meet Their Doom.' I considered our chances of survival if we became stranded on this slope. We were probably visible from the plateau below—but who would be coming up here at this point in the afternoon, when the park was closed?

"Spending the night on the peak without a tent or sleeping bags was not a great option. The idea of a rescue helicopter was embarrassing but comforting. I watched the smaller rocks roll down behind Julia's heels as she climbed and imagined the whole bed of rocks rolling downhill like a conveyor belt.

"This was officially dangerous, but there was no other way out. Even sitting and waiting would be dangerous if it went on long enough.

"We began to discuss the situation in a pretend casual tone.

"'Are you okay?'

"'Yeah. You?'

"'This way? What do you think?'

"'Not very good.'

"'Let's just keep going then.'

"'Okay.'

"The slope had changed from a half-pipe to a more convex, rounded surface. I felt like an ant climbing the side of an exercise ball. We finally reached a point when we couldn't find any footing secure enough to keep going up. I began to think about death. This wouldn't be a bad way to die, I thought, but it would be embarrassing.

"Maybe there would be a region of the afterworld for people who died doing stupid *extreme* things. We would be surrounded by base jumpers, rocketmen, and dirt-bikers. I didn't want to join this club for eternity.

"We clung to the mountain and considered our situation. The only way out was *up*. We took our chances and made our way in a diagonal ascending line, splitting the difference between up and down.

"The world around me faded. Other hills didn't matter. The ocean didn't matter. Everything else was background music for the task of moving carefully from rock to rock. Look at Julia. Look at my feet. Take a step. Look up. Take a step.

"Suddenly, we reached a green patch of scrubby, rough bushes. Labrador Tea, perhaps. The incline remained steep but now we had some purchase. Thank god for plants. We reached the peak only to find that it wasn't the top of the mountain but rather a ledge below the actual summit. Not that the summit was of any interest at this point. We snuck along the ledge, anchoring our steps in the fragile alpine vegetation.

"A few traverses of the gully wall and we had made it to the snow—home free. We began our descent. I looked down toward the bottom of the gully and saw our own tracks, clear dark lines in the snow.

"Yes, from here, our route up the side of the gully did look a little questionable.

"When we reached the wooden lookout with the sign, we broke into the crackers and smoked oysters. The platform was so perfectly flat and level. I was very happy to be there.

"I looked back at the peak. Nothing about it had changed, but it looked different to me now. No longer benign. No longer round and friendly. I had to admit it—this was a serious little mountain."

■

In Banff, Alberta, there is a similarly modest summit that has claimed more lives than many of the glamorous peaks that surround it. During the summers I worked there as a university student and then years later, when other assignments brought me back to Banff, I would go up Tunnel Mountain regularly. Shaped like a sleeping buffalo (its original name), Tunnel sits just above the town and the way up is nothing more than a 40-minute switchback that rises not quite 1,000 feet—a bracing jog with the dog. But at the top, it doesn't feel so domesticated. One must pay attention. The wind can suddenly pick up, and in the fall, when the path ices over it's possible to make the final hairpin turn, and slide right off the back of the mountain, plummeting down into the valley. Many have, especially the new arrivals in town, who like to drink five beers and then climb Tunnel in the dark.

On mountains and in families, the sunny safe plateau can change between one sentence and the next to something mortal. My father's death was like that—a quick, lucky fall that arrived at the end of a satisfactory day.

The Saskatchewan River

T HE LANDSCAPE underneath a big bridge tends to feature graffiti, debris, and used condoms. I had forgotten that. This wasn't the most appealing place for my father's ashes to end up.

Before he died, I had made a plan to drive through the prairies and see the bridge he had helped build in 1930. It was one of seven bridges that span the river that runs through the city of Saskatoon. My father graduated from the University of Saskatchewan as a civil engineer just as the Depression began. But the dean of engineering, C. J. Mackenzie, initiated a "relief project" that would employ as many men as possible and build something the city could use—a "bold, simple" bridge made of cement with nine graceful spans. My father was one of the team of engineers who worked on the bridge, which took 11 months of 24-hour labour, sometimes in the 40-below winter weather, to complete. It was a job he often talked about, with undisguised affection for "Dean Mackenzie," as he always called him. He was a paternal figure in his life, after losing his own father at the age of 12.

The completed bridge was more lovely than anyone could have predicted and it became the postcard icon of Saskatoon, its horizontal Eiffel Tower. I still have a photo of my dad in a dapper news cap, smiling with pride as he walks beside the tall, patrician Dean Mackenzie. I knew I had to make a trip back to the bridge and walk over it.

I flew to Saskatoon, where it was clear that the Broadway St. Bridge is the grandest thing about the pragmatic, farm-circled city. Close by was the Bessborough, a CPR hotel built in the days when they still resembled Scottish castles. I prowled through the grand, empty corridors of the Bessborough and then walked by the river to the base of the bridge. I had originally planned to scatter the ashes off the bridge itself, but it was high above the water, and that day the wind was too strong. The ashes might simply waft over to the forlorn parkette on the other side and coat the single park bench there.

Down by the pathway that wound along the riverbank, I found a bronze plaque almost overgrown by shrubbery that paid tribute to the engineering triumph of the structure. If I could scramble down the banks and surreptitiously pour the ashes into the river, this could be the official spot. Eyeing the current, I calculated that they would be carried under the bridge.

I had left behind the vase, thinking that a woman with a full urn on a bridge might draw attention. Public scattering tends to be illegal. The ashes, in a plastic bag with two garbage ties twisted around the top, were as heavy and big as two bricks. I had decanted the ashes from their original bag, which kept springing open, into a bigger one, a task I did as quickly and unthinkingly as possible. The ash was light grey, very fine, and clinging, except for the larger bits, which were honeycombed like bone marrow. Not like, but were. What does it matter if these are his ashes or just whatever was on the bottom of the crematorium, I thought, but I continued to address the vase as "dad." I put the new bag inside a dark blue velvet sack supplied to us by Just Cremation. It had a drawstring and reminded me of the old Seagram's bags we used to keep our marbles in.

The river was wide, a milk chocolate brown, with a steady, powerful current. The word Saskatchewan means "swiftly flowing river" in Cree, and one of its tributaries flows 1,200 miles, to the Bow Valley in Alberta. A good long ride. It gives breadth to the city and had dictated the scale and modest majesty of the bridge. In the public library I had found black-and-white photographs of its construction, how the supports were sunk in clay and the engineers had to compensate for the ferocious cold of winter which caused the materials to shrink. "Only four men died in the construction of the bridge," one news item reported.

I found a picture of three workers standing behind the rebar skeleton of the bridge's steel supports. One figure, not the tallest, wore a cloth cap that did not hide his ears, which stuck out, just like my dad's. The face was obscured, but there was a certain jaunty eagerness in the posture. I was convinced it was him.

My cousin Margaret Ann, from Colonsay, stood behind me on the riverbank. She didn't know my father well, being from my mother's side of the family, but she was kind enough to tour me around Saskatoon and to witness this increasingly odd ritual. The moment was awkward and unceremonial, but still, when I squatted by the water and looked up at the rib cage of the bridge, my mind filled with thoughts: of my father and mother skating on the river, which they loved to do; of my father working at the YMCA a few blocks away, typing the witty, flirtatious letters with which he wooed my mother; of my mother in the frame house on 10th St. wondering when my father would come home for dinner from the bridge-in-progress. Of my mother quitting her job as a switchboard operator, because the "relief project" hired only married men, and couples could only hold one job.

Traffic gleamed on the bridge, and my good shoes slipped on the stones at the water's edge. I untwisted the ties and tried to shuffle out the ashes, but they had been tamped down, and I had to dig them out. They sank, except for a few small clumps that caught on weeds, sticking like frog's eggs. I shook and shook the bag—it took a long time. Margaret Ann clicked her disposable camera. The fine grit got under my nails, and when I had emptied the bag I saw that my hand was grey, cadaver grey, gloved with the dust. I clambered back up the riverbank.

"Well, that's that," I said to my cousin, in my mother's words. She smiled and said nothing. Sentiment is not a prairie thing. We walked back to her car and drove past the city limits to the RV campground that she manages with her husband, in the great curving space west of Saskatoon. It had been farmland until the farms failed. Colonsay's grain elevator, one of the old wooden ones, was scheduled to come down soon. My hand, with its ghostly coating, lay radioactive beside me on the handle of the car door. Like having something stuck between my teeth, I urgently wanted the grit out from under my fingernails. But there was nothing to be done until we reached the campground, where I was staying in the guest trailer, a perfect, surreal bubble of shag-rug domesticity up on cement blocks.

Margaret Ann went back to the house to prepare dinner. Inside, I went over to the sink and turned on the taps. I watched the last filaments of grey dust run off my hand and down the sink as the trailer rocked a bit, buffeted by the soft, strong, constant prairie wind.

Be Home by Dinner

I'M THREE OR FOUR years old. We're living in a two-storey brick house on Stillwater Crescent, a dead-end street that peters out at the edge of Lake Ontario. On the other side of the bay are the smokestacks of the steel plants, with their tongues of flame. But they're a long way off, and the lake itself is huge. We swim in it in summer (until the polio epidemic hits), skate on it in winter. The lake lives alongside us like a large, gently breathing silver mammal that we all take for granted.

During the week, my father drives to work, through the small town of Burlington. My older brother Bruce rides his bike to school because there are no buses. Most days, it's just my mother and me, alone with the dogs. I have no idea how we spent our days. I can't come up with any memories of us doing things together, apart from ones I've reconstructed from photos in the family album. Perhaps this was because she was always there in the background: mother as weather.

My father came and went, which may explain why I have more distinct memories of him. The time I fell off Mrs. Perry's dock next door, down into the lake, and he caught the end of my long blond hair and hauled me back up in the air. I have a memory of sitting in his lap, in the armchair with the plushy red stripes. He's reading me Scrooge McDuck, our favourite comic, especially the part where he dives naked into a swimming pool full of money. When he was young, my father was a gifted cartoonist who had been offered a job with the Disney studios in the early days. But they couldn't pay for his trip down to California for an interview, and neither could he, so he stayed in Saskatoon and became an engineer instead.

We both loved reading comics.

My father drives home for lunch every day. Every day my mother prepares lunch, as well as dinner, including desserts for both. It might be just pudding, but cooked, not instant. Butterscotch or chocolate. I especially like the skin that forms on the pudding. One day we're at the table, I'm perhaps four years old, wearing my terrycloth slippers with the thick foam soles, and I want lunch to be over because *Small Types* is on. This is a radio program on CBC for kids. It includes a rather ghoulish traffic-safety jingle, sung in an operatic soprano:

> *Looook to the left, and loook to the right,*
> *And you'll never never get run ooooohver. . . .*

I hear the jingle come on, and ask my mother if I can please take my lunch into the living room to hear the rest of the program. She lets me, and I curl up in the chair beside the big furniture-sized radio, the plate balanced on one arm of the chair as I carefully tuck my slippers under me. But not carefully enough; one slipper catches the edge of the plate and it falls upside down on the rug, oozing sauce around the edges. My mother, at the end of some rope I have not detected, rushes into the living room, sees where her cooking has ended up, and spanks me.

This is out of character: my mother never shouts or hits. It's the first time I've been spanked and it makes me feel diminished and shamed. I creep up to my room. Later, I come to the top of the stairs and see my mother sitting in the big armchair. She looks troubled. Something about her long days on Stillwater Crescent alone in the house, and thinking about lunches, had clearly got the better of her. The spot on the rug has been cleaned but is still damp. She calls me down, and I climb onto her lap. An apology is extended, but not a satisfying one. I am quiet and dignified in my response.

It's my first glimpse behind the maternal curtain of someone I don't recognize, who isn't always mother.

When I was in my teens and precociously reading the British psychoanalyst and author R. D. Laing about the basic insanity of families, I took it upon myself to "cure" ours. I initiated social hugging. I hugged my parents whenever I arrived or left. They slowly adopted this new habit. They were devoted, loving parents, but physically undemonstrative.

When I grew up and had my son, I went the other way: I revelled in the physical intimacy of breastfeeding and caring for him. As he began to walk and climb, my body was the handiest set of monkey bars. He scaled me, swarmed me, inhabited me. In pictures of the two of us at this stage, he is always hanging off my neck and arm, like an ornament on a Christmas tree. I spent hours down on the rug with him, running a plastic car around a cardboard expressway, doing my best to make engine noises.

Our mothers were not down on the rug with us. They were too busy keeping house and stage-managing the world of home, with its scientific draperies and avocado-coloured appliances. They were putting on lipstick for the arrival of their husbands and wondering if 4 p.m. was too early to pour a biggish glass of sherry because they were bored and lonely. They played bridge. They joined school committees and pursued creative hobbies—my mother had many in her life, from ceramics to dressmaking. The children were part of this *mise en scène*, but not necessarily the central characters.

We had a washing machine with two hard rubber rollers mounted on top. After the clothes sloshed around in the tub part, my mother would feed the wet clean clothes, lump by heavy lump, through the rollers. They emerged from the other side thin and flat as cardboard, curving down into the laundry basket.

Don't get your hand caught in the rollers, my mother would always warn me.

■

We lived near a peninsula of homes, some quite grand, known as Indian Point. This wasn't a developer's moniker; the Mohawk chief Joseph Brant once had a settlement here, long before the smoke-stacks of Dofasco and Stelco arrived across the bay. My brother and I used to find arrowheads in the ravine. For the first years of my life, the way I spent my days was probably more Mohawk than mini-van. Okay, Joseph Brant didn't listen to *Small Types*. But I spent more time in the ravine than inside a car.

There were no other kids my age on Stillwater. We always had a dog on the go, and they ran free. Frisky, a border-collie/shepherd, was my brother's dog and my mother's favourite. Ricky (we had bad pet names, always), a cocker spaniel with weak hips, was mine.

The house had a coal furnace; once or twice a winter a delivery of coal roared through a basement window down a chute into a dark little room. Then my father shovelled it into the furnace. Milk and bread were delivered to the house too, left in the "milk box," an ingenious compartment that opened both ways, to the outside and inside. I am not really as old as Susannah Moodie but I do remember a horse-drawn cart hauling blocks of ice covered in sawdust. I used to feed apples to the ice man's horses. The warmth of the horse's breath on my hand.

Much time and labour were required to keep the household running smoothly. Home was a kind of theatre for the performance of family; curtains that opened and closed smoothly were important, as was the discreet box that covered the curtain-drawing mechanism—the valence. Parents focused on the material side of things rather than the inner life of their kids.

Mothers weren't expected to drive off to mom 'n' tot yoga classes. The job of preschoolers was to go outside and play, which is what I did. I went hunting for water rats down by the lake. I went next door to visit old Mrs. Perry, who would lend me her powerful binoculars so I could watch the fire spitting out of the steel-plant stacks across the bay. On weekends, my father might take my brother and me skating on the lake, and in the summer we would ride our bikes to the second hydro tower on the beach strip to swim. My mother swam, too, a fine figure in her black woollen suit.

There were no music lessons, no play dates, and, for that matter, no friends in my first five years. My brother occasionally deigned to let me hang around with him and his slightly delinquent friend Derek, as the two of them collected snakes and shot at things with their BB guns. You could order many wonderful things from the backs of comic books then: BB guns, Chihuahuas the size of teacups, bust enhancers, and sea monkeys.

So I had the ravine, the lake, my comic books, the company of two dogs plus some sea monkeys, and my mother, who was there but also absent in a way. Or just an adult. I remember her back, as she stood at the sink, or the stove, or sat curved over a panel of fabric at the sewing machine. Always making something.

My father worked for a company that manufactured pesticides and water-purifying chemicals. He was overseeing the construction of a new branch, which was the reason we had moved east from Saskatoon a year after I was born. Job transfers often determined the destiny of families in those days; Brian grew up in a Toronto suburb because his father, who worked in insurance, was transferred there from England. My mother had been whisked away from her own family to a strange new town and a house that my father had bought in the weeks before she arrived.

It must have been lonely for her at first. What I registered as a kind of emotional absence in those early years was probably nothing more than a current of depression, the isolated housewife's affliction.

Once I asked my mother if she had ever wanted to work at a career. "No, I was happy to stay home with you kids," she answered. Pause. "But I think I would make have made a good geneticist."

Too true.

"Oh, your mother's a smart one," my father liked to say with pride, whenever she produced some showcase dessert or upholstered a couch. He adored her. She was endlessly ingenious and artful in her homemaking. There was, however, the slightly disarming advice my father liked to give Casey, many years later: "Be sure you marry a girl who's smart—but not too smart."

There was no TV. I do remember the newsprint paint books with little dots; if you "painted" the dots with water, a thin wash of colour appeared. The radio was our main entertainment. I would lie in bed at night with a radio on beside me, the dial glowing orange, as I listened to *Bulldog Drummond*, *Dragnet*, and the *Amos 'n' Andy* shows. A few times, my father took me fishing down along the lakeshore. For some reason I longed for a bamboo fishing pole, and he bought me one. During the winter, he would take my brother and me iceboating on the frozen lake, a completely thrilling and dangerous activity involving bedsheet sails and two-by-fours mounted on skate blades. The three of us would go skimming and chattering across the goosebumped surface of the ice.

Nobody told me not to play in the ravine, or go down to the lake, or near the highway with the dogs. Nobody told me not to wander into construction sites, our preferred playground. The main rule was to be home by dinner. This was not negligent, this was normal. There was no preschool, no daycare, and no piano lessons, except for the occasional session with my grandmother, who raised her three children as a single mother by teaching piano.

If I was lonely, I didn't know it.

■

I like to catch frogs and bring them home, much like our cat likes to deposit gifts of mice on our doorstep. One day I bring a fine specimen back to the house and crouch on the stairs to watch the frog wetly lurch toward my mother, who is, as usual, standing at the sink. She steps back, almost on the frog, then turns and let out a gratifying little shriek. My turtle, however, meets a sadder fate. I let it roam about the kitchen floor one day when my mother passes through with laundry in her arms, obscuring her view of the floor. She steps on the turtle. Either the shell or the creature itself makes a very upsetting, high-pitched noise. Then it dies. So does Frisky, our best dog.

95

I am playing in the ravine with both dogs when he bounds ahead and darts across the highway. A pickup truck hits him, pushing his blond body forward as the driver brakes. He gets out and lifts the dog gently into the crib of the truck, which happens to be full of hay. He drives him to the vet, but they have to put him down.

I had wrapped my arms around Ricky but hadn't been able to save the better dog, the one my mother loved.

After the accident, in the kitchen, I try to normalize things. Bruce will really be surprised, I venture to my mother. She says nothing. I ask for a sandwich—lunch would surely help matters. She fixes a sandwich and plops it down in front of me. I eat it with a tight throat, as my mother goes upstairs without a word. After I finish, I creep up and see her lying sideways across the bed, face down, her shoes still on. I go back down to the kitchen.

■

Pet deaths were evidence that life wasn't kind, but it was mostly safe. "Play" meant roaming around our small town with friends, unsupervised. The task of parents was to construct a sturdy world in which these simple beings called children could grow up. The world outside was not considered perilous and toxic, as it is now. There were indeed pedophiles out there, penis-flogging losers, but if you didn't get into a car with them they were no threat. You could always take a different route home.

However, I was rummaging around in the basement recently and found a little pile of evidence that perhaps all was not right with my young, secure world. Some adolescent poetry and a few short stories from my high school yearbook. One, "The Eye of the Storm," was the story of a cartoonist on his way home to commit suicide. Another was called "The Lonely Road." ("A road is only lonely when someone walks down it," it begins, unpromisingly.) And oh, the poetry, the wretched, terrible poetry—beyond the usual puerility of teenage free verse: "Thoughts hang like rotten fruit in the room." This was the work of a smiling, flip-haired girl who didn't appear to have a care in the world—apart from this blighted subtext of Samuel Beckett-sized alienation.

My literary efforts were part of a phenomenon I call the Basements of Burlington. My mother did all her creative work in our large, cool, split-level, disorganized basement. Upstairs, she was mom. Downstairs, she was Georgia O'Keeffe. She had easels, paints, a potter's wheel, and a ceramic kiln in the basement. There was a ping-pong table where she laid out the tissue-paper patterns for her dressmaking. On the surface, her artwork was unsophisticated and craft-y; she favoured mother-and-child sculptures. One of her paintings was of a small blond girl with a rake, heading into a field of pumpkins. But there was something faintly threatening about those pumpkins. Her clay sculptures were unusual: in class, she was given the assignment to "sculpt your clay into an ordinary household object." She chose to make a blue hot water bottle, but in the firing the piece cracked. To keep it together, and as a kind of visual joke, she fashioned a set of grey skeletal fingers wrapped around it. Death's hot water bottle. Her ceramics teacher was left speechless by this object, and so was I.

Upstairs, the theatre of family ran smoothly, day after day. Downstairs, the basements of Burlington were devoted to pure, buried id.

■

A month before her 98th birthday, I went to visit my mother in her long-term care facility, where she had lived for two years.

"How's the book coming," she croaked. She had learned to ask what mattered to each of her children, even if she sometimes couldn't remember where we lived.

"It's plodding along," I said. "I've been trying to remember what it was like for you when we were living on Stillwater and you had just moved out east. What it was like for you to be a mother then." I was being offhand.

"Oh, I didn't think it mattered to you kids what I did," she said, "I didn't really think it was important."

Well. There you have it. She was spending her days and the prime of her life doing things she believed didn't matter, for people she thought didn't care. But she poured herself into it anyway.

By the next decade, this state of affairs became known as "the problem with no name," Betty Friedan's phrase for the loneliness of domestic life in the middle-class families of the 1950s.

The Great Unraveller

THERE IS SOMETHING about motherhood that undoes a woman, sooner or later, in one way or another. It's the Great Unraveller. Whenever you see someone who looks like a four-star parent, a composed, trim, confident woman picking up her daughter at the preschool on her way home from her demanding, high-paying but gratifying job, remember: you are seeing a mirage. Go home with her, shadow her, get into bed with her, spend a chilly hour in the park with the perfect mother and her child at dusk, and you'll see. Eventually she'll crack. She'll say, "Anthony, I *told* you not to do that! Now look what you've done! Are you satisfied?" in a tone of voice she loathes in other parents.

Or one evening, after too much Chardonnay, when her husband loiters too long on email after failing to unload the dishwasher, even after they had *discussed* this, there will be tears, shouts, and maybe something thrown.

The more perfect the mother, the harder they snap.

Independent women launched in fine careers sometimes fall madly in love with their small children, quit their jobs, stay at home, and cannot imagine going back to their old lives . . . until one day they wake up and find themselves alone, morosely sifting

99

sand on the desert island of modern motherhood—the atoll where women must be both church and state, extended clan and perfect play date, to their children. It is all up to them, because the real church and the real state like to pay lip service to the importance of child-raising, but when it comes to making life easier for mothers—preschool programs, affordable daycare, decent public schools—the church and state have better things to do.

In the past 40 years, family life has evolved. We have all-terrain baby vehicles. Fathers are more hands-on, while mothers blog and write more publicly about their rich, exasperating lives. Kids growing up are taking longer to leave home. But nothing fundamental about motherhood seems to have changed. Each mother breast-feeding her child is alone, with the glass of water just out of reach. And many mothers who shed salaries and worldly positions feel queerly, oddly isolated in their new and better lives at home, raising their children—surely the most important job in the world. Except that often it doesn't feel like that in the middle of it.

"Parenting" is a recent invention. In just two generations, we've gone from playpens (practical little cages for restless children, now viewed as abusive) to play dates (a four-way social encounter requiring scheduling, transportation, and alcohol). For the last decade, the dominant child-rearing wisdom has been that only total bonding, the near-fusion of mother and infant, can lay down the foundation of a healthy, successful adult. Somehow we have gone from ignoring the enormous sacrifices women made for their children in the past to valorizing a new and subtly sacrificial model of motherhood that, ironically, might not be helping our kids in the long run.

We work too hard at mothering. And we don't know when to stop. When Casey was 24 and looking for a GP in Montreal (no mean feat), I rustled up a few names from friends and emailed them to him. Along with the contacts for a couple of sound galleries

I had heard about that I thought he might want to check out . . . plus the name and number of a naturopath too.

"Thanks for the doctor referrals, I will check them out," he emailed back. "The galleries don't sound like my sort of thing. And when you give me too many resources at one time, it kind of stresses me out."

Our theories about the best way to raise kids have gone from the pre-Spock days, when the worst thing parents could do was to "spoil" a child with too much attention, through the post-war, post-Freudian focus on the importance of early childhood development to our current wave of "attachment parenting" and "intensive mothering," as it is known in the burgeoning field of maternal scholarship. Child-rearing, once something that new parents muddled through, has acquired a quasi-professional set of skills, accessories, and knowledge to become a culture unto itself. It used to be "Shut the door and let the baby cry"; now it's "Pick him up and never put him down," literally or figuratively.

I was a textbook intensive mother. I couldn't bear to "Ferberize" my son, which would mean . . . shutting the door and letting him cry himself to sleep. That was cruel! I was a human Jungle Gym for years and breastfed him for 22 months. Even in his twenties, I still hurt when he hurts; we share too many ancient neural circuits now for a completely clean separation. My mind may be elsewhere as he navigates his world in another city, but my nervous system is still attuned to his. Yes, I have a life, work, and an interesting husband, whom I love, but the unfolding of my son's fate, on good days and bad, can occupy my thoughts more than I care to admit.

This is probably not a good thing.

Intensive mothering arises innocently, of course, from intense love. But it seems based on the premise that children are inherently fragile vessels that require constant topping up with encouragement and self-esteem. As a result we've become the anti-Simon Cowells on the parental *American Idol* jury, always softening the blow of "no."

In the process, I think we've lost the middle ground between the too-distracted parent of the past and the overly invested, hovering modern one. One of the consequences of this has been a generation of twentysomethings perplexed by a world outside the family that plays by different rules. When they come through the door for a job interview, no one says, "You're on time! Well done!!!"

Judith Warner, a former columnist for the *New York Times*, published an appealingly indignant book in 2005 called *Perfect Madness: Motherhood in the Age of Anxiety*. She was addressing American, Walmart-sized anxieties, not the boutique levels of fear in Canada, but her book offers an aerial view of our child-rearing culture and clarifies just how quickly and radically parenting ideals have changed over the past half century. In the 1990s, middle-class mothers who could afford it began to interrupt or forgo their careers in order to stay home and raise their kids full time. Corporate moms torn between work guilt and home guilt, bumping up against the glass ceiling on the job and unwilling to work 60 hours a week to make law partner, began to opt out.

Since then, the job of mothering has acquired new dimensions and ambitions as a growing population of mothers choose to pour all their energies into it. (More fathers are tackling the stay-at-home role too. But less than five per cent of families are "run" by men.) Women began to make motherhood an all-consuming vocation in a way it never has been in the past, when homemakers had too many chores, and too many children, to focus exclusively on parenting.

But mothers are no longer managing the world of childhood from their distracted adult perch, phone in one hand, cigarette in the other; they're down on the floor and eye to eye with their kids, taking on the role of playmates, coaches, surrogate siblings, and all-round domestic CEOs. Mom looms large on the horizon now—

even more than she did in the pre-feminist past, when children were rug rats, not tender, complex little beings, and mothers had table-cloths to iron. No one wants to roll back down the hill into that world. (Too many tablecloths.) But the reigning "child-centred" theory of parenthood may prove to be less about the well-being of the child than we imagine.

Let us not forget, the full moon of motherhood has only been visible in the sky for the past 10 years or so. The intimate details of motherhood, now so bloggable, were once considered beneath discussion. In the 1950s and '60s, women were expected to pass through their child-rearing years as gracefully, stoically, and inconspicuously as possible; a new mother extolling the virtues of her Swedish breast pump at a cocktail party would soon find herself alone by the cheese tray.

When I had my son, in 1983, Mother Lit didn't exist. The myths surrounding motherhood were formidable and yet not well-artic-ulated. So the reality of motherhood, the intensity of the feelings combined with the 24-hour demands—this great reconstitution of the soul—came as a shock to the women of my generation. They had tasted some independence and didn't anticipate the *surrender-ing* that motherhood requires. The giving in and over that is part of the voluptuous joy of motherhood ran counter to the new feminist ideals of independence and self-assertion, ideals that suggested women must be harder, more like men, and *less available to others*.

Ironically, feminism in the 1960s neglected the spheres that most women lived in—the home and the family—to focus on careers, equal pay, and gaining entry to the working world of men. It took a few decades of guilt, conflict, and exhaustion for the women who were trying (and unavoidably failing) to balance work and family to discover that while the right to work is crucial, and for most families an economic necessity, careers, as turns out, aren't every-thing. Non-workaholic men sometimes figure this out too. Money makes the world go round but it doesn't assuage the heart.

All that has changed. The subject of motherhood is now on university curricula, alongside Hegel and postcolonialism. The first Museum of Motherhood will soon open in Seneca Falls, NY. Demeter Press, part of the pioneering Motherhood Initiative for Research and Community Involvement organization in Toronto, has published books on every possible social and cultural aspect of a topic that was once restricted to manuals on toilet training.

The great oppressor for the new mother—social isolation—has been vanquished by the Internet. No matter how far away the nearest neighbour is, she only needs to sit down at the laptop to connect with other mothers in the same boat.

In fact, the intimate nature of new motherhood, awash in all those bodily fluids and raw emotions, offers ideal material for our bare-and-share-all online conversations. Blogs and tweets are also well suited to the stolen-moment, ADHD reality of life with a new baby.

But mother blogs can also amplify doubts in the same way that symptom websites can feed hypochondria. The Internet has helped create the newly conspicuous culture of motherhood but it's also established a kind of apartheid policy. Perhaps the blogs flourish because motherhood is still a somewhat exotic island, not yet integrated into the larger social, economic, and political picture. The fact that online mothers share this "specialty interest," like people involved in animal rights or hang-gliding clubs, only betrays its still-questionable status.

Others would argue the opposite, that motherhood has become the bully on the block, with parents exercising a moral superiority over the childless. And what about the omnipresence of pregnancy and motherhood in the tabs, with all those arrows pointing to a possible celebrity "bump"? The actress who "puts her family first" and "loves being a mother more than anything else" has become the number one tabloid trope. Isn't that pop culture reflecting motherhood's shiny new status? Maybe. Or it could be just another way for us to obsess about women's bodies and weight issues.

To me, a "bump" on the tiny frame of Gwen Stefani is not really about a potential child; it's an acceptable form of fat. In the tabs, pregnancy is a Get Out of Jail Free card in the never-ending weight-loss stakes and a way for readers to track the pounds-on, pounds-off drama of "getting back in shape" after birth. A shot of a pregnant star wolfing down a bacon burger in public is not about self-indulgence but about "eating for two"—a *sacrifice* of her thin self to her growing baby. The pregnant movie star is an arresting contra-diction in terms, like Kirstie Alley pitching a line of diet products. We want our stars to be like us (to gain weight when pregnant) but also to live in a fairy tale (to have a flat stomach three weeks after giving birth).

The apotheosis of female celebrity has now become stardom + motherhood. What is more glamorous than being Angelina Jolie or Madonna? Being Angelina with a huge brood, biological and adopted. Being Madonna with a young Brazilian guy on one arm and a black baby on her hip. Presumably, they pursued mother-hood for their own reasons, not for the optics. But motherhood, once a frumpy, non-career-enhancing role, now only adds to their glamour.

This new breed of rich and famous mothers seems to look upon the job of raising children the way their own mothers might have once imagined careers—as something fulfilling, challenging, and slightly exotic. In terms of public perception, motherhood has become the Microsoft of life experiences, a respected brand of human software.

But this new status has also given birth (as it were) to a new source of anxiety. The more we invest in the mother role, the more pressure we put on ourselves to be accomplished, successful par-ents, raising accomplished, successful children. As boomer par-ents, we believe in self-expression, whether it manifests as art or narcissism. Our latest form of self-expression may be our children.

Every parent lives vicariously through the success or failures of their kids. But with more parents spending more time focused on child-rearing, the risk of over-investing in our offspring has gone up.

As usual with parental love, this has come about with the very best of intentions. Just as our own post-war parents worked hard to give us the material security and spacious rec rooms that their families couldn't afford, we did our best to shrink the generation gap and cultivate closer relationships with our children. We wanted them to be more like us—and for us to be more like our kids.

Motherhood now enjoys a cultural currency that it's never enjoyed before, but oddly enough our *knowledge* of children, what's best for them, doesn't seem to have kept pace. Childhood itself is a relatively recent invention; for most of the 19th century children were thought of as a source of cheap labour or adults-to-be, better "seen and not heard." They helped on the farm or were raised by governesses in the nursery, well apart from the adult world of their parents. Children were not considered fascinating. They were spanked, rebuked, and yelled at. They were held upside down and slapped on the bum at birth or circumcised without anesthesia as infants. This was not considered cruel because no one attributed consciousness to babies. It's only in the past several decades that we have paid attention to vital issues such as pain in children, the impact of absent fathers, or the enduring wounds caused by childhood sexual abuse. We're only *beginning* to fathom the depths of childhood.

In the meantime, we are anxious parents. In the pre-dawn hours, mothers camp out in lawn chairs to get a spot in the desired preschool. They haul themselves up the park slide with the same single-mindedness their feminist mothers once brought to climbing the corporate ladder. It seemed to make so much sense at first, to work less and be there more for our kids. But now the pressure's on, to be the best possible mom and to produce the best possible kid.

This is not the fault of mothers. I see this as a new manifestation of the same problem that bedevilled motherhood when I was new to it, back in 1983: the role of raising kids, which women mostly shoulder, had been largely neglected by my generation of feminists. Gradually, some of us had children and changed our tune. Women began to write and talk more honestly about the experience of mothering. Then popular culture seized upon it and exalted it to an almost religious status, until movie-star motherhood became something even more desirable than fame. And movie-star mothers generated new maternal myths by showing none of the wear and tear of raising kids, because they're able to pay for maids, nannies, and personal trainers. But for 99.8 percent of mothers, the job is still a frustrating, anonymous, and unglamorous one because women not only still do most of the scut work; they must also stand in for a more caring, humanist world as well.

In *Perfect Madness*, Judith Warner is nostalgic for the time she spent as a mother in France, with its maternal postnatal visits and free daycare. She never got over her return to America, where daycare is still as pie-in-the-sky as universal health care. In Canada, when Prime Minister Stephen Harper announced the government would cut the funding for international aid, including family planning programs, there was an uproar. Giving women the ability to space their pregnancies would probably protect their health more directly than other more expensive aid schemes. Governments in North American continue to imagine that family just happens and kids just grow, outside the frame of things that really matter.

The new chicness of motherhood is only superficial; at the end of the day, the mother often finds herself alone, mildly if unfairly resentful of her non-breastfeeding partner, and suddenly a non-player in the economy. So she works even harder at mothering, to make her job more interesting, more valuable. This can rob the family of ease, playfulness, and peace. There's too much trying. A mother's lucky if she has a supportive, solvent partner and a few girlfriends going through the same thing.

But the modern mother's unsolved anger continues to be instructive, shedding light on the true valence of children and families in our world. How shocking it was to hear Barack Obama, early in his presidential campaign, deliver a speech that emphasized the importance of fathers to family life, especially for young black men. When was the last time a presidential candidate put fatherhood on the political agenda?

The anxieties around child-rearing have escalated at the same time that the collapsing economy has made family-friendly work arrangements less likely. The recession affected more men than women, with the result that many at-home mothers now have to seek out the more plentiful service jobs. A woman out job-hunting in the current climate is not going to insist on a flexible work schedule when there are others willing to work on any terms.

But the market is not and has never been a kindly place that cares about the well-being of families. It is a mill that grinds on, and parents are at a disadvantage. It's easier for a camel to pass through the eye of a needle than it is for a mother to finesse both a career and a family. "Having it all," that 1990s mirage, now sounds like a ridiculous goal, part of the greed that got us into environmental debt.

There may be an upside to the Great Recession of recent years, though; unemployed and laid-off parents are spending more time at home with their children. Perhaps not in the best of moods. There has been a rise in the numbers of stay-at-home fathers too. If they can manage to keep a roof over their heads, the consequences for families might not all be negative. What children lose in terms of music lessons they might gain hanging around with mothers and fathers who suddenly find themselves rich in time.

■

Our generation of parents cultivated self-expression, community, and relationships in general. We travelled for years and postponed the real world. We went to therapists to shrink our superegos and took drugs to expand our minds. We were amiably alienated from our poor parents, who were only trying to create a safe world in the aftermath of two world wars and the Depression.

But our mothers and fathers didn't sit on the couch and watch movies with us or text us twice a day when we broke up with our boyfriends. They weren't our buddies. They were, in our eyes, materialistic, hard-working, out-of-it grown-ups who lived in a different world from us. Our values were better values, we thought, and our relationships were more authentic.

We were, in a word, arrogant. Arrogance is a blind spot; when you have it, you cannot see what you're not seeing.

As a result, my generation of parents (I am trying to avoid the rather nautical-sounding word "boomer" here) has cultivated more intimate relationships with our kids. Along with that has come our deeper *identification* with our kids. We ride the roller coaster with them. We hold their hands, even when they're 23 and law school turns them down.

One of the criticisms often levelled at boomers has been our betrayal of the optimism and ideals that we once believed in. Somewhere along the way, we gave up and got interested in granite countertops and organic wine instead. But I think our idealism didn't go out, it just went underground, like a root fire—and when we had children, our hopes for the future were rekindled. We are ferocious in our efforts to protect our kids from the big bad world (with its lead-poisoned hockey sticks). The gap now is not between the generations. It's between the hothouse domestic realm and the world outside of the family—the reality gap.

So parents chauffeur their teenagers to all extracurricular activities, banish potential allergens from the family menu, and sandbag the household against the rampant dangers outside. The world may well be more dangerous than it was 50 years ago, but my mother's generation faced wars and polio epidemics without instilling fear in us.

No wonder many twentysomethings graduate from college ill-equipped to deal with rejection, self-determination, and engagement with a world that feels hostile just because it's not patting them on the back. They are oversensitive to criticism and, at the same time, too hard on themselves when they aim high and fail.

I went to my doctor the other day and ran into a friend who was in the waiting room with her 28-year-old daughter, keeping her company. That made me feel better for having just mailed an asthma puffer to Montreal, for my coughing 25-year-old son.

And now we have no idea whether this most-mothered generation of children will benefit from all the attention—or rebound in some unpredictable way.

Although his critics on the right saw Dr. Spock as the promulgator of "permissive parenting" (the beginning of the end of civilization, in their view), in fact he believed in establishing firm boundaries between parents and children. At adult parties, children ate at a card table in the kitchen, not sitting on their mom's lap eating crostini and salmon roe. There was an offhandedness to Spock's advice that suggested children were sturdy, independent organisms who didn't require constant coddling and brain stimulation in order to establish a sense of self. The worlds of adult and children had not yet overlapped and meshed to the degree they are today.

It's hardly surprising that we identify so closely with our kids as they negotiate their twenties. The sexual revolution of the 1960s and '70s was not about growing up faster; it was about enshrining the "inner child" and perpetuating a childlike innocence. It was about face-painting, daisies, and blowing bubbles under cloudless skies. In its more serious expressions, it was also about protesting the loss of young lives in imperialist wars. We wanted respect for the young, and for the uncorrupted child in all of us. *Not* growing up became a virtue.

"Much of what we do these days in the name of perfect motherhood," Warner writes, "is really about 'reparenting ourselves.'"

What is missing in the mother-literature is more political perspective. The real problem with motherhood is not about getting your partner to empty the dishwasher; it's about recognition and support in a concrete way, from governments and the economy, for the job of raising children. Nothing much has changed about the experience of motherhood, it seems, except the outfits and the equipment.

Motherhood remains the Great Unraveller, the thing that sooner or later brings a woman face to face with herself. The power and joy of motherhood continue to outstrip our little ideologies. No matter how our theories about motherhood evolve, the raw daily experience of it continues to ambush each new generation of women, in good and bad ways.

And just when you think you've got a handle on it, it slips through your fingers again. For mothers, graduation day never comes.

111

The Degree

C ONVOCATION at McGill takes place under white tents,
on the green lawns of the downtown campus, at the end of
May. The weather can still be raw, which it was the weekend we attended. But after six years of ambivalence about university and a great deal of hard work Casey had earned his degree in
history, and I thought it was something worth celebrating. Even
if no one else in the family did.

Brian had spent the last few weeks in France, reporting from
the Cannes Film Festival; he had just arrived back, jet-lagged and
exhausted. In any case, ritual gatherings and convocations hold little appeal for him. He had skipped his own graduation, in fact. As
for Casey, when I phoned him earlier to talk about plans, he wasn't
sure he wanted to go to the ceremony, or indeed what the point of
it was.

Was I going to have to use a forklift to get everyone mobi-
lized—and for what? Once again, I felt like I was singlehandedly
trying to create a "family moment" in a vacuum. The train ride
to Montreal with my semi-comatose husband was not very festive.
There was no "Remember when he was in Miss Archer's class and
made that clever bridge out of toothpicks?"

But our ragged clan did assemble, on an overcast day with a cold wind that shivered the blossoms on the trees. As soon as we arrived in Montreal, Brian came down with a fever and a sore throat. He closed the curtains in our lovely hotel room and crawled under the covers. Casey and I had dinner in a restaurant down the street. The next day Brian announced that he was too sick to attend the ceremonies.

"Being sick never kept you from showing up for band gigs," I reminded him meanly. This father-and-son dismissal of social ritual (as I primly thought of it) was wearing thin. It also made me feel like the boring CEO of the family, trying to wrangle everyone into the stockholders' meeting.

But fine, I said, you stay in bed. No, I insist. I'll go sit through the entire alphabet by myself. From under the covers, Brian replied that he'd try to show up later.

Casey Burke Marley Johnson. (Yes, that Bob Marley. No wonder he didn't want to go to dental college.) I calculated that the Js would arrive roughly in the middle of several hours spent sitting on hard folding chairs in an unheated tent, watching polished young people, many going on to post-grad work in lucrative fields of study, cross the stage in their book-shaped caps and Oxonian robes.

I reached the campus in good time, I thought, only to discover that more diligent families had staked out their seats near the stage hours earlier. I found an empty chair toward the back and reserved it with my coat. Then I went behind the tent and followed the long serpentine line of grads until I spotted Casey, in his bachelor robe with the white fur around the hood (the "arts" fur) and a tasselled cap perched on his springy hair. Always a sucker for costumes, he was getting in the spirit of things. He was wearing his Ray-Bans, too, even though the day was overcast.

Casey had only thought to invite his girlfriend, Rebecca, and his roommates the night before so he wasn't sure they would turn up. Wow, good sense of occasion, I thought glumly. At least our party of two wouldn't need to make special reservations for lunch.

I went back to my chair under the Big Top. Families were milling about the lawns, getting yearbooks signed and taking photographs, as the girls' high heels sank into the grass. Nobody in our family cares about this occasion except me, I thought morosely and . . . why *did* I care again? I had forgotten. And come to think of it, why hadn't I pursued a career as a cabaret singer like Marianne Faithful?

Then I saw Brian striding across the lawn with a scarf around his neck, carrying a large tea.

"I took some Advils," he said, sitting down beside me.

I studied the program and counted the list of arts graduates. Three hundred and sixty-five. But I had to admit that whoever announced the names of the students as each one came to the stage was giving it his all.

Thomas . . . William . . . Cullen . . . Please come forward!

There is something about an unadorned list of names that is mysteriously moving. The Vietnam Veterans Memorial, that long black granite wall, got it right. Every time a new name was announced and another grad crossed the stage, a pocket of cheers would rise up from their family in the crowd. Tears came to my eyes, and I didn't know why; it was the wedding moment, of witnessing hope and promise, while knowing that life will test that hope in ways that couldn't be imagined now.

Finally Casey was inside the tent, a few yards from the edge of the platform. He craned around in the line, spotted us in the crowd, and waved. He was still wearing his Ray-Bans and grinning. James Dean, B.A. I assumed he would pocket the sunglasses before he crossed the stage but, no, he left them on, loping across the platform and warmly shaking the chancellor's hand with both hands, like T. Bone Burnett getting an award at the Grammies.

I thought this tiny act of subversion was harmless enough, but months later we learned that it had set a historical precedent;

henceforth, the wearing of sunglasses was officially banned from McGill Convocation exercises.

Well, it wasn't a fellowship but it did represent a contribution to the academic world.

Rebecca and several other friends had showed up just in time to watch Casey cross the stage. They whistled and whooped; heading off stage, Casey waved the paper baton of his diploma in the air—he had graduated "With Distinction," which was news to me—and flashed his smile. I insisted on witnessing the rest of the students right down to Zwicker, and then we gathered on the lawn. Brian's hue was slowly changing from grey to pink, now that the captive-audience part was over. Even the spring sun had made an appearance.

116   We took pictures of our son and his friends, then of him riding his bike around the lawn in robe, cap, and sunglasses.

"I get it now," Casey said to us, who also likes a good wedding. "Thanks for coming."

After the ceremony, we took the group out for lunch at a sunny, high-ceilinged bistro on Bernard Ave. There were other families there as well, celebrating, and solo diners reading newspapers on the patio. It was the sort of Montreal place where Sunday brunch goes on for hours, as if Monday will never arrive.

Love Trouble

AFTER GRADUATION, Casey stayed in Montreal, where Rebecca was still finishing her degree. The pickings were slim on the work front but eventually he found a minimum wage job with a francophone sound and light production company, in the rigging department. Being *le chef des moteurs* was about as far as he could get from the lecture halls of McGill, but he did hang on to one shred of school—his weekly late-night show on the college radio station and his host persona as the Rock and Roll Doctor.

My chronic motherhood didn't extend to staying up 'til 1 a.m. to listen to the live broadcasts, but I tuned into the podcasts online, which had acquired a small but loyal following. I liked the music (unsurprising, since some of it came directly from our basement) and his retro beatnik slogans. ("The show that puts the wildness in your mildness.") For maternal surveillance purposes, the mood of the program was also an excellent barometer of how things were going for him in his new post-grad world.

(I had been warned not to eavesdrop on his Facebook page, a familiar parental form of spying. But since he is also one of my "friends," I do get his status updates. "Casey is a dork," he posted one afternoon when I was logged in. "Is this genetic?" I commented. "Possibly," he posted back.)

That long, cold winter, I noticed the playlists on his show were changing their tone. The ratio of Roy Orbison to zydeco was going up, and he wasn't playing as much Ramones. Instead, there were more early, crackly sounding blues by Lucille Bogan and lots of Sam Cooke, especially *A Change Is Gonna Come*. I didn't think he liked Amy Winehouse but he made an exception for a killer demo of her singing *Love Is a Losing Game*.

It soon became evident to me from the musical offerings on Rock and Roll Radio that all was not well in the romance department.

■

Rebecca was younger than Casey, just 21. A beautiful girl from a big, warm family. We had met her a few times and liked her. Wow, good for him, I thought. The two of them fell for each other, and then six months later things began to unravel. I'm not sure what the problem was, apart from the basic, insoluble problem of being in love in the first place, and Casey was too discreet to go into details. But his efforts to sound okay on the phone were not always successful. He was having doubts, and she didn't want him to have any doubts. All I knew was that they seemed to be working awfully hard to be happy.

I tried to remember that all I had to do was answer the phone, put things in perspective for him, and not be pulled off balance myself.

At which I failed.

■

Well, I'm not getting very far with this part. I don't know how to write about my son's love troubles, and shouldn't even go there. But *not* to write about them in some way would eliminate the thing that probably affected me the most about this particular stage of growing up. There's nothing sadder than the sound of ruined love in your child's voice. For a parent, this is new terrain. We can proof-read their essays and buy them duvets but we can't put love back together for them.

Love trouble is the signal that the most gratifying stage of motherhood, when you could actually *protect* your child from being hurt, is over. He's out in bad weather on his own now. It's your job to listen, to sound optimistic, and to feel helpless. Also, when you hear yourself saying, "Are you getting to the gym?" make a note: better hit the gym yourself.

■

It was February or March. Another call from Montreal. They had broken up, again, and he was determined to make it stick this time. I was attempting to be brisk and normal. He said he hadn't been outside yet but that he planned to. He was going to fix his bike.

"Just keep moving," I said. "Today won't be good. But it will get better, I promise you."

"Okay. Thanks."

We hung up. A wave of sadness descended. I have not quite lied, although I could have elaborated: it does get better, but it is never the same again, not really, and even a mother with several decades between her and the first or last departing love can feel the sting again.

Drugs, Music,
and Sex in 1968

1968. It was only a year since I had finally shed the last of my tattered virginity, the same spring and summer I smoked marijuana for the first time, listened to *Sgt. Pepper's Lonely Hearts Club Band*, and rose up the staircase of that last, long crescendo that ends "A Day in the Life." The Beatles had gone from singing bouncy little ditties like "Love Me Do" to performing neuroscience on my brain.

In my last year of university, drugs and the new music had just made their way to Toronto from San Francisco and London. From the Canadian prairies too: Neil Young and Joni Mitchell played at The Riverboat. The Jefferson Airplane came to town; Bob Dylan was at his most beautiful, long before the pencil moustache. He had just put out *John Wesley Harding*. My boyfriend's apartment balcony overlooked Yorkville Avenue, where there was a bad-trip trailer parked down the street.

He and his pals liked to drop acid on the weekends, sometimes in the course of sleepover parties in one parental home or another (minus the parents). When they got stoned they would often conduct a shock-and-awe tour of the furniture. One item that sent them onto the floor in paroxysms of glee was a transparent hassock with a bed of artificial flowers inside. It did cry out for ridicule.

But on the whole, dope wasn't my cup of tea. It took me another 10 years before I got up the nerve to try acid (and found it less gestalt-shifting than mescaline). My Burlington brain preferred alcohol. So I drank scotch and water and puffed on the occasional joint while everyone else, including the more intrepid girlfriends, took tabs of Windowpane or Purple Microdot. They marvelled at the hassock, too, or sat with glistening eyes while the boys fell about laughing. I could enter into the spirit of things but I wasn't actually seeing the molecules of the shower curtains writhe and dance. *Seventeen* magazine hadn't prepared me for this sort of dating situation.

While my boyfriend took acid and toured the universe, I rode along in the sidecar, adept at contact highs but still intact, suburban, afraid. It was going to be love that cracked me open, not a chemical.

As a result, I sometimes found these weekends a little . . . taxing. A night at the movies and then home to bed would have been just as mind-expanding. But I didn't complain. It was understood that the collective experience was more important, more fun, than most of the things that couples did on their own: dates, for instance. Dates were old-fashioned. We wanted to experience the new consciousness as a group, to bounce around on it together like a trampoline.

But underneath the giddiness there was also a more momentous sense of being on a genuine frontier. This was new. Nobody thought about where the experience might take us or what we could make of it; that was what "the system" did, boxing up the future. *We want the world and we want it now.* Our job was to be in the moment.

Unfortunately, smoking marijuana tended to pluck me *out* of the moment, not into it. ("Wow, my heart is beating fast. Maybe my aortic valve is leaking. . . .") But sometimes getting stoned did feel like a revelation—an irrefutable, visceral sense of what *could* be. Since then, decades of avid horticulture have bred stronger strains, but there were times when the gentle dope of the day made me think: yes, this is how I ought to feel *all the time*, this plush connection to the low hum of life in everything.

For my poetry-writing boyfriend, I think drugs were exactly what they were meant to be: an X-ray that exposed hidden truths. A do-si-do of the *weltanschauung*. Getting stoned wasn't just about lying around listening to *Dark Side of the Moon* and falling madly in love with the patterns in the rug. Marijuana still had an aura of sacrament about it. We were initiates into another avenue of higher education.

It's hard to imagine now, but drug use was not part of the mainstream, and "rehab" was something you had to do if you broke a leg. Before the 1960s, only Thelonius Monk and beatniks smoked weed. Until grass, mushrooms, and acid came along, our culture of intoxication didn't go far beyond a case of Molson's Blue on the dock. Alcohol wasn't as much of a fixture on the scene as it is now. Binge-drinking was still Skid Row behaviour, not a prom-night ritual.

Long before weed, however, there was speed, a dangerous but curiously tolerated drug. When my mother went to her GP in the 1950s complaining about weight gain and a lack of "pep," the doctor routinely prescribed amphetamines.

"You should have seen me run around with the vacuum," she recalled with a certain relish. Speed was around the way antihistamines are now. Some writers thrived on it: Jean-Paul Sartre wrote voluminously on speed; Jack Kerouac famously tried typing on one long scroll of paper so he wouldn't have to stop to roll in a new page.

But speed didn't deconstruct your world view; it just kicked it up a notch. It gave people energy they didn't actually have. Acid and marijuana, on the other hand, rearranged the whole grammar of things and melted down the words.

To point out the obvious, dope and acid fed a lot of the new music as well—not just the lyrics, but the perceptions that woke

123

up language. *Sgt. Pepper's Lonely Hearts Club Band* is one long pipe dream, the album that revolutionized pop music. (A year later came the song "Ob-La-Di," a tune John Lennon referred to as "Paul's granny shit," but never mind.)

Drugs fought cliché until they began to generate their own. Getting stoned can become a case of chasing the dragon, trying to recapture that initial visionary rush. But for a brief time—in the late '60s and early '70s—I think we had it: that first, fresh uncorrupted glimpse.

Not that we were so original or groundbreaking; it was mostly a matter of being the right age at the right time. There was an assumption that smoking dope or taking acid was not just a lark but a new *technology*, a way to draw aside the curtains of the ordinary world. It didn't feel like escapism; it felt more like tuning in, Timothy's Leary imperative. Turn on, tune in, drop out.

Leary was not, in the end, the best advertisement for the long-term effects of taking acid, having turned into a sort of Joan Rivers of enlightenment toward the end of his life. Aldous Huxley exited more gracefully. His last words, to his wife, were "LSD. 100 Micrograms I.M.," to which she responded by injecting him with the requested amount.

In 1968 taking drugs wasn't considered seedy; getting stoned was almost an act of civic hygiene, like volunteering at a food bank. It was about *seeing*, and *seeing through*, the rules, hypocrisies, and convention our generation had all grown up with—values that had helped our parents raise protected, secure, well-fed, well-educated children, who then grew up to become questing, idealistic, naïve, self-involved, and somewhat careless young adults, unconcerned about careers or making pots of money. My friends joined CUSO or signed up for Katimavik. They drove Volkswagen vans overland to India, and slept in hammocks on the beach in Mexico. Marriage, houses, and having children were postponed until the last possible moment.

We didn't worry about the future; indeed, it rarely crossed our minds. It was taken for granted that we could invent our own futures in a world that was environmentally and economically well-disposed toward us. The young were golden. Nothing stood in our way—jobs grew on trees, travel was dirt cheap, the war in Vietnam was troublesome and probably immoral, but self-contained. The world was still intact, and so were we.

All the more reason to take it apart, along with our consciousness.

This enterprise, however, had some grave consequences. A girl I knew in university took acid and began to experience one orgasm after another, like a set of rapids, and it wouldn't stop. She had a breakdown and disappeared. Acid probably contributed to the suicide of two other friends. The term "mind-blowing" wasn't accidental.

In our son's growing-up, I think Casey preferred Jamaican overproof to smoking dope. We never had to go through chats with the principal or the drug busts and showdowns that are a rite of passage for many parents. No, the irony in our family is that drugs were probably more important in our lives than they have been in our son's.

But music was an even more defining force. This was before pop culture became the great hairy beast it is today. Even in 1968, when rock 'n' roll was 12 years old, the new music was still relatively self-contained, an upstart genre in a world of classical music, bland ballads, and *Masterpiece Theatre.*

I remember the night that rock 'n' roll first breached TV, in 1956, when Elvis Presley appeared on *The Ed Sullivan Show.* As my mother and I sat in the den watching Elvis sing "Don't Be Cruel" and "Hound Dog," I felt a blush of embarrassment; we were watching something sexual together, on the television, which had never happened before.

And well before the civil rights movement, even though the

face of rock 'n' roll was mostly white, it was rooted in black culture—in gospel, R&B, and the southern blues that the Rolling Stones emulated and made popular. Unlike the rest of society, the early televised dance concerts, like *The T.A.M.I. Show*, were racially integrated.

Open-air rock shows like Woodstock and the Stones' Hyde Park show in London were new. Many of us had grown up in nuclear, secular families in the suburbs and had never experienced a sense of community on that scale. Drugs, music, political activism, and the sheer demographics of the postwar baby boom created a culture that we felt we was ours, and ours alone.

Music had a political voice then too. On May 4, 1970, when students protested Nixon's plans to bomb Cambodia, National Guardsmen opened fire on the protesters and killed four of them. Neil Young's song "Ohio" came out a week later, a song full of anger and pain that hit like a passionate editorial.

But as Young reflected in a 2008 interview with *Uncut* magazine, "It's a different world now than it was in the 1960s. I am not under any misconception that my next record is going to change the world." The headline for this story was "Rock's last great battle cry."

The great bonding experience for our parents' generation was the Second World War and its jittery aftermath. For us, it was the new music. It mirrored us—and it excluded our parents. That was sort of the point.

The role of the arts shifted, too, from a marginal, high-brow pursuit to something that felt more urgent, relevant, and personal. *The Battle of Algiers, Revolver, Exile on Main Street, Astral Weeks, Blonde on Blonde*, Jackson Pollock's action paintings, Jean Luc Godard's movies, The Living Theatre's performances—these weren't *divertissements*, they were works that challenged and changed the rules of their particular medium. Art also began to take on a more political role, charged with uncovering the truth in a buttoned-down era that was full of elisions, hypocrisies, and constrictions.

The culture of the 1950s tried to construct a safe, controlled world, whose buried fears nevertheless found expression in the Cold War, with its bizarre domestic accessory, the fallout shelter. It was an era with little interest in sexual expression or social justice. The civil rights movement was still to come. The closet was not just for homosexuals; it was a crowded, dark place filled with female poets, secret Buddhist meditators and suburban teenage girls like me, who thought there must be more to life than mastering touch typing, wearing crinolines, and tolerating sweet but silent boyfriends.

Since I wasn't up to full-blown rebellion, art was the only acceptable way out of innocent, upholstered Burlington in the '50s; that's why I lay on the dining room rug listening to Charlie Mingus records, read the existentialists, and took a suitcase full of poetry to summer camp. That's why I got on the bus to Toronto see the exhibit of mildly erotic paintings by Robert Markle and others at the Dorothy Cameron Gallery, before the police shut it down.

Now, of course, there's no need to get on a bus to find the edge of pop culture; you can't open your email without being forced to wade through it. The *New York Times* and the tabloids have converged in the middle, both eager to report on the "news" of a drunken celebrity who drives up on someone's lawn. The boundaries of visual art have become fluid and permeable; a work of art is just as likely to be a business deal (Damien Hirst's paycheque) or a display in a department store window. Art is a shoe. Women's shoes are self-help. ("I'm worth a $595 pair of platform booties.")

The days of one homogeneous culture that reflects the prevailing political winds are gone. Pop culture, protean and ever-changing, now scintillates in a million little pieces. The recording industry has collapsed, atomizing into self-marketing ventures and musicians who earn their living online or on tour. The combined worlds of TV, music, and social media have become a hall of mirrors, a Babylon of self-expression, a chorus of cooing, like pigeons in the grass. It's fertile and febrile and maybe healthy in the end—I'm trying to avoid Codgerville here—but the scene is so mercurial. I can't figure out how anyone makes money online, unless they sell their coffee tables on Craigslist.

Meanwhile, our lives are simultaneously more connected and more isolated, as we tunnel from one suburb of the web to another. Potential artists have access to an audience of billions long before they can figure out if they have anything to say.

Okay, that does sound codgerish. But the creativity of the new generation is difficult to evaluate because it's so raw and evolving. Something more twitter than Twitter will have come along by the time you read this quaintly jet-lagged book. Art has become more about audience, less about artifact. Everybody's first drafts are out there, topped and tailed with great-looking credits. We're all thinking out loud, en masse.

Pop culture now irradiates us from every side, like a vast tanning salon. But in the 1960s, especially in music, there was an outburst of energy, non-conformity, and self-expression that was idiotic in some aspects (I won't quote Donovan although I have upon occasion) but it also helped define us.

Our parents didn't like it or want to be part of it. Rock 'n' roll was "jungle music" (note the racism). So music was our crucible.

Now whole families buy tickets to Springsteen concerts or share downloads of K'naan. Ads selling electronic equipment show silver-haired men playing air guitar. Is there a male left on the planet who does *not* play guitar? Casey listens to one or two genres of music that we don't have the stamina or wardrobe for, but on the whole our two generations bathe in the same murky Ganges of pop culture.

Our son's musical palette is deeper and broader than ours was but it doesn't necessarily define community for him. There are so many musical genres now that they've become a badge of personal identity: shoegazer bands vs. ambient-doom-metal. Indie is no longer short for "independent." But in many cultural ways, our two generations have meshed. What is his and his alone? I'm not sure. It will be something he spots on the horizon that we can't see. Something his parents can't understand.

That would be interesting for all of us.

■

Our relationship to our parents was markedly different. We had a proprietary sense of seeing through the world of our "materialistic" parents. Protest music, rock 'n' roll, the exploration of the psyche, the new science of consciousness—these were *our ideas*. India's 10,000 years of spiritual practice or William Blake's universe in a grain of sand? Our discovery. We were as engorged as ticks with a sense of being the first generation to see things *as they really were*.

Our families lived, we thought, in benighted stupefaction while we were all waking up. Even as we drank our parents' scotch, we made fun of their crystal decanters. I did, however, secretly admire my parents' attention to tradition, their seasonal centrepieces and silver carving knives. I viewed their domesticity from an anthropological distance, and with a prescient nostalgia: I knew early on that I would not live like them. In many ways, I felt claustrophobic about family, but I was also hungry for more.

■

The big divider between generations, though, was the so-called sexual revolution. The birth control pill made the ludicrous notion of "free love" possible at the same time that it cleared the path for more sexually transmitted diseases. For women, the choice to have sex or not no longer pivoted around wanting children or fearing pregnancy; it became a choice based on sexual pleasure or "exploring relationships." We wanted to become not just equal to men in freedom of choice (jolly good) but *similar* to men in as many ways as possible (a bad idea and unattainable). Second-wave feminism—a surfer term, I believe—suffered from an implicit sexism of its own; it undervalued the traditionally feminine spheres of housekeeping, caregiving, and motherhood. It targeted the male paradigm of that era instead; let's all become competitive, job-identified workaholics with no close friends!

I think of it as "the sexual devolution."

I took the pill for a year or two but it made me depressed, so I went back to using the moronic but straightforward diaphragm. In London, the National Health supplied me with one, but I had to go through a bizarre "fitting" overseen by a nurse in a clinic. I had to demonstrate proper insertion of the little latex boat. I was afraid the thing would slip out of my grasp and fly off across the room, which they often did.

The diaphragm is a fallible device—wellies for the cervix—but at least it doesn't mess with your hormones, suppress ovulation, increase your risk of blood clots, or give you suicidal levels of PMS. I was leery of the pill from the start (and wrote a gloomy harbinger of its potential consequences that a women's magazine declined to publish because it wasn't sufficiently upbeat).

It was very nice not to worry about getting pregnant, a relief not to have to resort to abortion, but the sexual revolution came at a price: chlamydia, gonorrhea, pelvic inflammatory disease, urinary infections, all the afflictions that the unprotected female reproductive system, on the pill, became vulnerable to. Multiple partners without condoms was a new experiment and basically it failed. Thousands of women were left infertile from infections caused by an intrauterine device, the fiendish-looking Dalkon Shield—another freedom appliance we embraced too eagerly. (The women sued and won. Small consolation.)

And what about the heart? Was "sleeping around" good for women? That was another failed experiment, if you ask me. When sex is severed from the possibility of pregnancy, it alters the whole geography of intimacy. The stakes are lowered; the mystery train pulls out of the station. "No regrets, Coyote. . . ." (Speak for yourself, Joni. *Je regrette beaucoup*.) Free love was a sweet deal for the men (give or take a case of non-specific urethritis) but it was disastrous for women's sexual health and maybe their peace of mind too. How many of us lumbered through our twenties on Clydesdale-sized doses of Premarin? How many of us compromised our fertility in order to make ourselves available to the next guy in our life—old What's-His-Name?

The pill freed us to behave just like guys. So much for feminism.

It's my theory that the womb doesn't like a lot of traffic. It raises the risk of cervical cancer, among other things. It's men with their billions of sperm who biologically lean toward the scattershot approach. They're the spendthrift gender that has an urge to spread the seed in order to ensure that one or two plucky sperm fall into the right, hospitable vaginas and find their way to bingo. There's a lot of collateral damage when it comes to sperm—it takes a village, including the village idiots. But women are born with every egg already numbered and unique. When ovulation is thwarted (the logic of the pill), the orientation of the female body and mind is radically altered. The unique dialect of pheromones falls silent; some studies have shown that men are less attracted to women on the pill because the chemistry of ovulation is missing. Other studies reveal that lap dancers get more tips when they're ovulating.

A woman unafraid of getting pregnant with the wrong man has lost a portion of her good sense and connection to nature, her body, herself.

This isn't really an anti-contraception rant, much as it begins to sound like one. I don't think biology is destiny. But biology is a sweet, integral part of our female identity, and the reproductive narrative, whether it's expressed or latent, is part of our forward momentum in life. When we lose the biological signals, obscure them with chemical decoys, ignore the cycles of ovulation and receptivity, we may be losing the top notes and bass lines of our body's music.

Women who feel armoured and invulnerable in their bodies are going to be less forgiving of their potential mates, less attuned to the men who somehow become irresistible to us, despite their flaws—when the stakes are high and the chemistry is right.

Genes call to genes. Our bodies dance with one another in ways we don't understand. Chemical contraception might suppress more than our fertility; it might also muffle the dialogue between the biological body and the social self.

I don't think this kind of wild-eyed, pro-ovulatory thinking will necessarily lead to an increase in 15-year-old mothers either. The more attuned to their bodies women can become, the more likely they are to take responsibility for avoiding unwanted pregnancies. Using chemical contraception is like putting on a hazmat suit; it creates a false sense of inviolability. It overrides the notion of consequence. And without consequence, sex becomes a monologue.

Okay, let me pause for a moment to wipe the flecks of foam from the corners of my mouth.

I could also put it this way: I might have had a second child if my fertility hadn't been compromised as a result of "the sexual devolution."

■

In 1968, all these factors—the pill, the new music, and recreational drugs amplified the importance of choice, self-expression, and individual freedom. These values felt like progress after the post-war drive to hunker down, buy bigger refrigerators, and stabilize society. And for a time they were.

Most of all, there were the numbers. In 1971, the average age of the population in North America was 26. There were so many of us that no matter how crazy we acted, we always had company.

Incidentally, I still believe that we can see the universe in a grain of sand. Mr. Blake was right about that. It's just harder to get to the beach these days.

Long-Term Care

MY MOTHER'S FACILITY sits at the end of a street called Corporate Drive, at the northern rim of Burlington. A suburb of a suburb of a suburb. As I drive toward it, the pink and grey building looks pale as a mirage, as if it's slowly vanishing, like its residents.

I park in front with my usual mixed emotions. I look forward each visit to seeing her 97-year-old face and to spending time with her. But it's the new drifting mother, not my regular old one. She takes some getting used to.

I press the code that opens the doors and keeps the forgetful ones from wandering. I'm relieved when the woman at the front desk doesn't look up as I sign in. There's enough forced merriment in here.

The St. Patrick's Day clover leaves have come down from the bulletin boards, and the bunny-and-daffodil Easter decorations have gone up. I suspect these are more a form of occupational therapy for the staff, because I've never seen any resident of my mother's wing looking at them.

For one thing, most are belted into wheelchairs, well below the level of the notice boards. For another, many are lost in their own little wildernesses. If they don't arrive in one, they soon build their own. When I pass through the common room, one or two of them might chant, "Help me . . . help me." Like the rabbit in that camp song ("In a cottage in a wood/a little deer at the window stood. . . ."). They don't say it loudly or urgently because they know not to expect rescue. And the staff, most of whom are kind and patient, know to ignore their chant or else to lean in close to the new one, pat her knee, and clearly say, "Eleanor, you're fine."

There is no actual emergency. It's just that some unquenchable part of their brains continues to be alarmed at their predicament, of finding themselves old and powerless.

It's surprising how easily one acquires armour here. I breeze in through the sun-filled day room, where the residents gather each day in their cones of isolation. Today there is a newcomer sitting in a wheelchair by the windows, with down booties on her feet. She sits closest to the budgie in the cage. "Please," she murmurs as I pass by, smiling. She's not where she is used to being.

"Hello!" I say, smiling at her. I use the same bright inflections as the staff now.

I spy a familiar resident in a saucy striped sweater as she toe-creeps down the hall in her wheelchair.

"Hello, Mabel!" Mabel likes to roam, using her slippered feet to slowly pedal her way up and down the corridors. She doesn't speak but she has clear eyes and a steady, knowing gaze. That's because she hasn't been here long, she hasn't gone inside herself yet. Mabel gives me a foxy smile as she passes by. I wish I knew what she was thinking. I zip into my mother's room, where two of the staff are helping her do the transfer from bed to wheelchair via a complicated block-and-tackle device hooked to the ceiling. I retreat to the corridor to let them finish.

Sometimes I like to visit in the evenings, when the residents are all in bed and my mother is lying in her nightie with her hair fanned on the pillow. Her face is soft and beautiful when she is lying down. Also, our roles are clear-cut: she is in bed, while I am the mobile, capable one, pulling up a chair. She also likes the cozy noise of the staff moving through the corridors, wheeling the snack trolley from room to room.

One night I sailed in.

"Oh, I'm so glad you're here," she said rather gaily. "I was just trying to think of ways to commit suicide that wouldn't reflect badly on the family."

This didn't faze me. It was like a Sudoku puzzle for her—a problem to put her mind to.

"Yes," she went on, "it's not easy when I can't get up, you know. I could take the drugs off the carts when they go by, but that would be hard for me to manage, and I wouldn't want the staff to get in trouble either."

"Why are you thinking about this?"

She flipped her hands, one of them covered in plum-coloured bruises. I think she bangs them against the bed rails in her sleep.

"Oh, I'm so useless like this. I'm tired of being such a burden on everyone."

"You're not a burden. I think you make life easier for the staff because at least you can kid around with them."

"Well, yes, that's something. And they wouldn't have jobs if we weren't here."

"So you are being useful. You're giving people jobs."

"That's right. I do think of that sometimes. I was just having a gloomy moment tonight I guess. So you picked a good time to come."

Then she demonstrated how she could still reach over, ever so slowly, and find the switch on her lamp. She turned it on and off, twice. And that was a better moment.

In the corridor, I hear the staff murmuring as they tend to my mother. The halls are lined with colourful prints. Most are pictures of flowers, in vases or fields, but another theme is crueller: empty chairs at tables for two, on the deserted patios of some vaguely French or Italian café. At the end of each corridor are sunny nooks with artificial flowers, plug-in fireplaces, and faux Victorian armchairs. It really is very pleasant here, I remind myself, except that the main activity is dwindling, and everything that precedes dying. Sometimes that too.

Inside her room, the walls are ringed by photographs of her three children and three grandsons. My sister Jori hangs the pictures and keeps things homey. She is a hairdresser, among other things, and cuts my mother's hair. After my father died, she and her family moved in with my mother, into our old family home, and lived with her for three years. It was hard on everyone. My mother couldn't accommodate another household, one she wasn't in charge of, swirling around her. The lawyer who drew up her estate when this plan was hatched gently warned us; families tend to fall apart under the strain of elder care, he said. Oh that won't happen to us, we laughed, we all get along.

A year later, my sister, the gentlest, kindest person in the world, was shocked to discover the anger she could feel toward someone she loved. My powerful mother was teetering through the house like a stilt walker on Benadryl; any day she was going to fall and break something. So the glacial process began of researching homes, along with the endless paperwork and scheduling of social worker visits, while we convinced my mother that this was a good and necessary decision. It was too hard for Jori and her husband and son to be a family with my mother still trying to rule the roost. The three of them spent most of their time sequestered down in the rec room while she sat alone upstairs. Everyone was living under the same roof in deepening estrangement.

My mother remembers this phase, dimly. "Jori and I had different ideas about decorating" is how she puts it. Or "I've never known anyone who loves to shop like Jori," to explain why my sister had to regularly flee the house to avoid committing matricide.

It is to my sister's credit that they both survived the transition from the tensions of the family home to the flat horizon of the institutional bedroom. Jori continues her kindnesses, visiting her almost daily. My sister paints, as well. One of her pictures, a watercolour of blue hollyhocks, hangs opposite my mother, and although her eyesight is almost gone she still takes pleasure in it. Jori is the hero of this story.

My brother Bruce and sister-in-law Kathy take care of my mother's financial and medical details, and visit every Saturday. They monitor her 17 medications. I show up on Sunday afternoons, having spent the hour's drive from Toronto playing loud music to get pumped. You need to bring energy into this place or it will take it from you. I have to keep reminding myself that this is only normal, and we were lucky to find a bed in such an affordable, pleasant place.

"She's ready for you now," says Samuel, the easygoing male attendant whom my mother rather likes. I go back into her room.

Someone has dressed her in a pink plaid shirt today, with the blue fleece vest and the stretchy grey pants that don't quite hide the dread ruffle of the diaper. I pull her vest down to cover that, more for my sake than hers. It's not an outfit my mother would have chosen, but it means that someone here is paying attention. Someone wants her to look nice.

The line between night and day, inside and outside, life and death is blurring. The staff used to lace her feet into her old walking shoes every day. Despite her not walking. Now she wears a pair of shapeless blue slippers. We're not even sure where they came from. When I point this out to my mother and ask about her lost shoes, she waves a hand and says airily, "Oh I don't care about that.

I don't care about anything anymore, except my children and my grandchildren."

I kiss my mother on her dry forehead, noting as usual that her eyes and the skin around them look inflamed. Nobody can figure out what the problem is. Her blues eyes stare into the middle distance, unfocused; she has just enough vision left to dimly register what I'm wearing.

"You've had a lot of wear out of that top," she'll say. Or "That's a good colour on you."

But she can no longer scrutinize me too closely, I realize, with a guilty sense of relief. Her fading vision maroons her in long days unrelieved by books or TV. A year ago, she broke her hip shortly after moving here. She survived the surgery but never walked again. She still plans to, though, every day.

"I was up for a while this morning," she'll report, or "If I use the railings in the hall I think that will get me going." We don't contradict her.

The staff wheels her into the dining room for breakfast, lunch, and dinner. She eats them all. Everyone revels in her appetite. She sits at a table with Mary, a totem of sadness who never speaks, and with Windy, a handsome old man with beseeching eyes who dearly longs to speak but can't. She likes Windy. In between the meals, she sleeps, her head supported by a horseshoe-shaped neck rest, or she sits in her wheelchair facing the open door of her room, "waiting for some action," she says, and "watching everybody else work."

She's learned the drill here: don't complain, stay on the good side of the staff, and count your blessings. The Celexa and clonazapine don't hurt either.

I keep my mantra going: my mother's not in pain. And after a bout of depression after her hip surgery, she's no longer in anguish.

"The staff is friendly here," she says. "It's amazing how you can get used to having men dress you."

Or "I'm lucky that I can always nap," she tells me gamely. Then, with more anger, "I nap, and nap, and nap!"

My mother is frighteningly cogent at times and confused at others. This is a boon. It doesn't pay to be completely alert in her situation. She is the oldest person in her wing and yet one of the most responsive. She can still evaluate her decline.

"My brain's going," she tells me. "I can feel it. It's terrible."

Sometimes she complains about her eyes, that they feel gritty. Today I decide to try the Chinese herbal eye drops again, standing behind her with the tiny vial. This is always the cue for her to squeeze her eyes shut.

"Open this eye, just a bit." No response.

"Mom, you need to open your eyes so I can get this stuff in." One eye blinks open for an instant. I pinch the plastic bottle, the eye snaps shut again, the drops roll down her cheek. I try the other eye, and the same thing happens. Oh well. Maybe some got in. Mentally, I shrug. It's difficult not to, in this place of decline. I imagine the staff must think this too.

That's good enough.

"Shall we go for a spin down the hall?" I ask, as if this were a new and brilliant idea, instead of the only thing we can do in here. Going outside, into the pretty courtyard, is too bright for her, too disorienting.

"Yes!" she says firmly. I find myself almost excited by the prospect of these miniature expeditions—trundling to the end of one hall, then the other. I look forward to them. It's as if we're setting out to view Victoria Falls.

After the voyage comes tea time. I roll her into the dining room and position her with her dominant hand, the left, close to the table. I pour two inches of coffee with milk in a cup—more and it will spill. Her hand moves tremblingly and in slow motion toward the cup, and she raises it to her lips. She always squeezes her eyes shut as she drinks for some reason. Then the hand with the cup slowly, slowly, moves back toward the edge of the table. A moment of suspense as I watch her navigate the edge of the table, but she locates the saucer with the bottom of her cup and it's done. The sip is accomplished. I place a cookie where her hand will find it.

"The cookies are always good here," she often remarks. It's true, sometimes they are homemade, although I don't know by whom. Her feet are elevated in the wheelchair; I stroke her swollen ankles, which are taut and swirly with pale colours, purple and red. I make mindless small talk. Real talk about my real life doesn't engage her any longer. When I talk about Casey, she might rally. "Oh, isn't that wonderful," she'll say, or "Be sure and give him a big fat kiss for me."

But this afternoon, she is drifting more than usual.

"Do we have a mother?" she suddenly asks, looking straight at me. Okay, a not-cogent moment.

"No, your mother died some time ago," I say, not adding, "And you're my mother and you're still alive."

"Yes, I know, but did our dad remarry?"

"No, he didn't. He died too. Actually, he died before your mother did."

"Oh. I thought he might have remarried."

Over by the budgie's cage, the new resident begins her gentle chant.

"*Help me.*"

I get up and clear the dishes, to make some noise.

"Shall we go for another walk?"

"Sure, why not!"

I propel her all the way down to the end of the east wing, where two of the staff are sitting in the empty nook.

"Hello, Olive!" says Samuel.

"It's odd at first," my mother remarks when he is out of earshot, "but you can get used to a man taking care of you. And sometimes they're gentler."

Other times she will say, "I keep thinking there's a man around somewhere." This is not surprising, after spending 68 years with my father. "I still wake up in night and try to move quietly, as if he's beside me in the bed," she adds, wistfully. Another staff member, a woman with curly black extensions, detours over to my mother. "Hello, grandma!" she says, coming in close to her face. "Hello, blue eyes!" She chuckles and walks away. I pivot my mother's chair around, and we begin the journey to the other end of the hall.

"That's how they all talk to you here," says my mother in a carefully neutral voice. It doesn't pay to complain, it's best to be a good sport—but I catch the subtext. The staff banters with the residents who can still respond, but sometimes it's like they're ruffling the fur on a dog or talking nonsense to an infant. With so many residents to care for and the rapid turnover, it's easy to lose track of who's still inside their body or who has fled.

I start to push her toward the west wing, where the daycare kids next door are out in the playground. This is a big draw for people out shopping for a facility; they imagine their mother or father sitting at the windows, drawn by the sound of children nearby. It's a nice concept. But no one looks or cares. The noise and bother of children is behind them now. Even the "therapy cats" that wander the halls go neglected. The staff hangs cat toys from the railings for the resident pets so they don't get bored.

Instead, the residents mostly sit, trundle, or assemble like ghosts for dinner at 4:30 in the afternoon. Their eyes follow you like runaways hiding in the woods. Most are on sedatives of some sort. Which makes sense.

"They're all very friendly in here," my mother keeps telling me, as if I'm here for the first or second time. "They treat you quite well," she says, "although you have to wait. You have to wait for everything."

"Well, there's not enough staff to go around," I say, as I always do. "I guess you've had to learn how to be patient in here." I start to push her back toward her room.

"I'll say. I'm so patient now it's ridiculous."

My smart, salty mother.

■

When I was three or four, our household went through a flurry of entering contests. With my father's help, I entered a contest to name a blond cocker spaniel (which was the prize). But the name Blondie proved to be not creative enough. Then my mother entered a contest to name a new Betty Crocker cake mix and she won. She called it "Candle Glow Cake Mix," and before long a box containing a mink coat was delivered to our door. It was what was known as a "shorty" coat, waist-length, a lustrous brown, with deeply cuffed sleeves and a cool, silky lining. My mother wore it as her "good coat" for the next 15 years.

By the time I was in university the fur on the cuffs had worn thin, so she cut off the sleeves and turned the coat into a vest for me. These were the days of Sonny and Cher, with Sonny's fur bolero. Or the Mamas and the Papas, with John Philips's ridiculous Dr. Seuss fur hat. The politics of wearing animals hadn't yet arrived.

My mother had left the vest unlined. It was nothing but many small pelts stitched together. When the seams began to shred, I relegated it to canoe trips, where it became indispensable, slightly fetishistic, and not at all out of place in the woods. I have snapshots of me wearing the fur vest over a plaid flannel shirt, with a large compass hanging around my neck, as I study a topographical map. *Très sauvage.*

Eventually the stitching on the vest gave out, but once again my mother salvaged more bits of the Candle Glow coat and transformed the discarded cuffs into an old-fashioned muff for me, a kind of open-ended purse. Out of other scraps, she sewed a fur headband and a detachable fur collar. I occasionally wrapped both around my head, turban-style (Simone de Beauvoir's worst legacy to women). Then she cut the bedraggled remnants of the vest into thin strips of mink. These she glued onto a black wool waistcoat, creating a strange and wonderful fur-striped garment that was part Star Trek, part Art Deco.

I wore it over a black turtleneck when I was feeling particularly antic. There was no other piece of clothing in the world like it.

Then, in a spasm of good taste, I pushed the vest to the back of my closet. It didn't surface until one weekend when Casey was home from college and I was editing my old clothes. Throwing out the 1973 blue corduroy Betsey Johnson jumpsuit finally. I handed him the fur vest. This might be something the Rock and Roll Doctor would like to wear on the air, I joked. Casey immediately saw the potential juju in this item and took possession of it.

He went back to Montreal and wore it "live" for his next radio show. The fur vest, he reported, had definitely boosted his musical healing powers.

Then Halloween came along; once again the garment was pressed into service. One of his roommates borrowed it and was tagged wearing it in party photos. The vest looked pretty good on him too.

I know my mother would be happy to see this last bit of her imagination and handiwork, still out there, dancing.

■

During the week, I phone each night around 7 p.m. Sometimes she feels compelled to call us during the day, but it's not often she can navigate the buttons on the phone. She has an ongoing sense that I'm never at home; it's true, sometimes my work takes me away for weeks at a time. This is faintly scandalous to her and has left a residue of anxiety about my whereabouts and my marriage.

But there are days when she manages to push the right buttons on the phone. Brian took a call from her recently.

"Oh, Brian, it's Olive. I just wanted to let Marni know where I am," she lightly informed him.

"Hi, Olive," he said, unflummoxed. "And where are you?"

"I'm in the Presbyterian church," she went on, "in case she comes looking for me."

The next time I saw her, I gently corrected her.

"Why did you tell Brian that you were at the Presbyterian church?"

"Well, I was!" she said indignantly.

Maybe one of the staff had wheeled her downstairs to a church service, I thought.

"But we belonged to the United Church. That's where we used to go, when we did go to church. Why wouldn't you go there?"

"The Presbyterian church always had more going on," she explained a bit sadly. Ah, the road not taken.

Lately she has been talking about her own mother and father.

"More and more when I wake up or go to sleep, I find myself thinking about Mother and Dad."

"Good thoughts?" I'm always scavenging for family secrets.

"Oh, all good. I think they were wonderful parents." Then another question occurs to her.

"Is the big white house still there?"

I know what she means; the big white house is the house she grew up in, on 10th St. in Saskatoon.

"Yes, it's still there," I say.

"That was such a good house," my mother says firmly. "I always think that if ever I wander off and get lost here, I'll just make my way to the white house."

I tell her this sounds like a sensible plan.

146

Another time I am visiting in February. My mother's gaze drifts away from my face more often now. "And how are you liking married life," she once asked cheerily, forgetting that I've been with Brian for 31 years.

Today I find her, sleeping in her wheelchair, the padded support around her neck. I take a moment to just look at her, before the role-playing begins. Then she opens her eyes and registers my presence. I bathe her face with a washcloth, like a baby. I like any bit of physical comfort I can give her because the social part gets weird. So I water her, then I water the azalea and poinsettia on the windowsill. On the dresser is a giant Valentine's card from my sister—so big my mother can still see it, or at least the shape of it, from her bed. Smart.

"Your nose is running a little," I point out.

"Oh it always runs now," she says. "It's going to win all the races."

We go down the hall, to the windows and the sitting nook. The light sometimes hurts her eyes, but today there is a soft February light, with clouds in a blue sky—puffy, perfect Simpsons-cartoon clouds. Two streets over, the suburban development stops and there are real trees, even a few tall white pines. Scraps of the old rural Burlington are still visible here. I babble inanities about the weather, the traffic, the houses in the area.

"Look at those beautiful clouds in the sky," my mother says. I wasn't sure she could see them.

"Yes, they are beautiful."

Then I talked about Brian's mother, who is 91. Doing well, but plagued by chronic back pain. Having to spend half her days in bed now.

"Well, it's the same for all of us," my mother opines, "it's just old age. We're on the edge."

"That's right. Nobody gets out of here alive."

"We all come to the same bitter end," she said with a proud little toss of her head.

"Well, you know, it could be quite pleasant. You might be sleeping and one minute you're dreaming and next minute, whoosh, you're outta here."

"Let's hope."

◼

At 7 p.m., when I make my nightly call to my mother, it feels like I'm lowering a rope and a bucket down a well—I never know if she'll manage to bring the receiver to her ear. Often, the staff has already settled her for the night. They raise the bars on the sides of the bed. This means she's not always within reach of the phone on the night table beside her. Rolling over, stretching her arm, lifting the receiver—it's all epic for her. So whenever I call, I let it ring seven, eight, nine times. Often, if she gets the phone out of the cradle, she will drop it. A period of noisy fumbling and laboured breathing follows, as she hauls the thing up by the cord. I feel a vicarious surge of pride when she gets the receiver to her ear, like a parent watching her child perform on the parallel bars.

"Thanks for calling," she always makes a point of saying, before we hang up. "Have a good night," I always say, both of us well aware of mornings that might not arrive.

But there are nights when the phone is too far away and she has to lie there and let it ring. Or the phone drops and she can't retrieve it, so it stays off the hook, the dial tone droning, my line engaged. The staff will be busy or chatting down in the common room, their charges finally tucked away for the night. If the phone isn't off the hook, I hang up, wait, and try again in 10 minutes. But on some nights the phone is near enough, and her hand finds it.

I hear her speak into the receiver in a wavering but strong voice that is no longer sure who or what will greet her.

"Hello?"

The Broken Year

I T WAS MID-OCTOBER, still warm, with that gold late-
afternoon light. Too beautiful a day to drive, I decided when
I stepped outside with my car keys. Besides, the bike would
be faster. I was hurrying to a yoga class, part of my new regime.
The rat race of relaxing! I could still make it, I thought, if I didn't
go back inside the house to get my helmet and panniers. Twinge
of guilt over that. Then I slung my workout bag over the handlebars and set off.

As I spun along Carlton Street in high gear my mind spun along
too, toggling between life and work—not a great leap in my case.
What if, what if, and then, and then . . . Distracted, I only noticed
the glitter of broken glass in my path at the last minute. Ride
through it or around? I swerved. That must have been when the
cloth bag swung over into the spokes of the front wheel; in any
case, something sent me flying over the handlebars until my face
hit the pavement. I felt the right lens of my glasses press, press into
my eye socket and braced for it to shatter. Amazingly, it didn't.

Now I'm really going to be late, I thought.

I tried to get up, but my right arm in the sleeve of my black
jacket wouldn't move. Oh well, let it rest there. I rolled over and lay

in a Corpse Pose. Street yoga. A dark-haired man in a navy blazer stepped off the curb and knelt beside me.

"Don't move," he said, "you'll be okay." He flipped open his phone and called 911, as pedestrians gawked.

Another good citizen extracted a key from my pocket and locked my bunged-up bicycle to a post.

"I'll stay with you 'til the ambulance comes," said the Samaritan, who had a deep voice and a professional manner, as if he tended to falling cyclists on a regular basis. (He turned out to be the general manager of Fran's restaurant.) He called Brian and left an impeccable message, even though I knew that my husband was at a meeting, with his phone turned off. Lying there with cars detouring around me, I felt surprisingly comfortable and relaxed—the genius of shock.

I tend to agree with Freud that there are no pure accidents. They're more likely to happen when the under-brain is wrestling with some problem. Later, when I replayed the accident in my mind, there was a moment in mid-air when a supercilious voice in my head said, "Yes! This makes perfect sense." My fall felt like a choreographed expression of the off-kilter state I had been in for some time. The surrender of flying through the air made me realize how tightly I had been holding on to everything. Trying not to let go.

■

The funny thing was that I thought I had already weathered the letting-go phase of motherhood when Casey went off to college. He seemed so independent, earning his own money, yet we were still in touch, etc. But it turned out that the genuine pulling apart was only underway now, when he was 24. The numeral doesn't really matter; it could be 14 or 29. And for me the letting go was tapping into some old, broken places.

The summer and the push-pull with Casey at the cottage had been difficult. I wasn't sure whether he was going through ordinary early-twenties angst—the kind I went through and thought I wouldn't survive—or something more fixable that I ought to fix. I began waking up every day at 6 a.m., with the same tape-loop running in my head: *Am I being too hands off or too meddling? Should I email him the names of a counsellor/antidepressant/naturopath/indie record producer, or would that just bug his ass?*

The Mother Tapes, wobbly and stretched from being played over and over.

Brian was getting pretty tired of the tapes too, which he heard second-hand, at 7 a.m. After all, it wasn't as if Casey was trapped in an SUV that had just plunged off a bridge. He was not playing Second Life in a mouldy basement room or pursuing an obsessive email relationship with a 42-year-old bipolar schoolteacher in Georgia. He was just working through a difficult romance, wondering how to make a living with a B.A. in history and figuring out what he needed (or didn't need) from his parents. Growing up, in other words.

But he was taking things hard and had a cough he couldn't shake. ("No resilience," said the textbook voice in my head.) It was his voice on the phone, gallant, trying not to complain, that spun me down.

So I mailed him some vitamin D. I ordered him a full-spectrum desk lamp, for Seasonal Affective Disorder ("You are a funny person," he emailed, when this sizable appliance arrived at his door). I had thought that at my age I would be looking back on the bygone, roiling emotions of family life in crone-like tranquillity. Instead, here I was still hovering, like a new mom in the ICU.

Maybe the neural circuits that fire up when you have a baby never entirely fizzle out, I thought; the mysterious symbiosis that makes a mother wake up full seconds before her newborn even starts to cry falls dormant as he grows up—but can still be roused, years later, *in extremis*. The phone rings, you have a sinking premonition it's your sister with bad news, and it turns out to be

THE BROKEN YEAR

true. The soldier's mother sits bolt upright in the middle of the night, knowing something is wrong. Not so unusual. Why else would we send prayers to people, if we didn't think they reached them?

"That's crazy," Brian observed crisply when I ventured this theory. Our tolerance for nutty behaviour is high in this household, but "hearing voices" or "channelling moods" is not acceptable.

The more pedestrian explanation was that I was not, in fact, a marvellously sensitive satellite dish of a mother. Instead, as my son pried himself out of the family bosom, I was having a wave of separation anxiety (my specialty) and projecting my own panic about what would become of me onto him. His reasonable concerns about his future were stirring up old, irrational fears in me—ones I hadn't dealt with yet.

My problem, not his.

So a friend recommended a therapist, a mother of grown kids herself. The year before, I'd already done some cognitive-behavioural counselling, a bunch of "strategies" that help keep your thoughts from swerving over into the worry ditch. Which was useful too. I was doing some meditation (although the nasal New England inflections of the voice on my meditation tape could be profoundly irritating. . . . "*As best you can, focus on the breath at your nostrils . . .*"). I was going to yoga. Sandbagging the levees all round to keep the flood waters at bay. I knew my levels of self-involvement were dangerously high, but *not* thinking through all this wasn't the answer either. I had to "work with the murk."

■

I cradled my limp right arm with my left, like a sleeping cat. The paramedics arrived and sat me up in the ambulance; they seemed a trifle bored by this middle-aged, helmetless woman who had managed to fall off her bike without even touching a car. One arm of my glasses was broken (not a good look), a cut on my brow was bleeding, there was a gash on my calf. They asked me which hospital I wanted to go to.

"Isn't St. Mike's the best place for trauma?" I said brightly, hoping to engage their professional side. It was also three blocks away. Off we sped.

The ER of St. Michael's Hospital is indeed a trauma centre that also deals with the inner-city cases, the smashed-up drunks and the mentally precarious. A whole crew was milling about the waiting room when I joined them. The paramedics fetched some ice for my elbow. I was in pain by this point and feeling sick but on the whole impressed by my sang-froid; my old habit of rehearsing worst-case scenarios really comes into its own in these situations.

I left another message for Brian, then called a friend, Janet, and asked her if she felt like hanging out in ER for the next five or six hours. I could have a concussion and I didn't trust my judgment; if they recommended the Whipple Procedure (an operation that basically removes all your internal organs, then puts them back in again), I wanted some backup.

All the nurses and doctors on duty that evening, I noticed, were unusually good-looking. Had I wandered onto the set of a medical sitcom by accident? At last my name was called, and I was wheeled away to be X-rayed. Then a handsome young doctor (or actor?) ushered me into a cubicle. Janet arrived, then Brian. Brian was jolly and not overly concerned, until he looked at my elbow.

"Oh, that doesn't look right," he murmured, blanching.

I inspected it; the elbow was bulbous and lavender-coloured, a Popeye elbow. He helped me shed my jeans so the doctor could clean up my leg. Then I was given a couple Percocets and a prognosis: I had fractured three bones in my elbow and would need surgery, which might involve "some plates and pins." I would regain the use of my arm, although perhaps not full mobility. Would I like to book into St. Mike's and wait for surgery—there was a bed available—or go home and mull over my options?

As full of medical opinions as I was, I knew nothing about elbows. There was also a good chance that a surgeon at this hospital would look like Robert Downey Jr.; everyone else did. So I admitted myself and was wheeled off to an older wing of the hospital, gloomy as a 19th-century asylum. The operation would take place as soon as they could schedule a surgeon, they said, which might take a few days.

When I arrived at my room I saw an older woman with a wild corona of white hair sitting on the edge of her bed. She was holding onto her knees and talking, her robe agape. Oh dear, I thought, my roommate. I was in too much pain to be social, but she spoke to me anyway. When I pulled the privacy curtains across, she went on talking, softly and steadily.

Her name was Gwen. She had diabetes, a deep foot wound, something implanted in her upper arm, and she was almost blind. But she was very upbeat. I never did figure out what she was in for. By that time, it was close to midnight. Brian went home, and I fell into a Percocet sleep.

Sometime during the night I woke up. I noticed that Gwen had turned herself around and was sleeping with her head at the foot of the bed, facing the door, which was open. The light from the hall shone on my bed. I closed the door.

"Please, leave it open," Gwen said in a little voice. I did. The next morning, she apologized.

"It's because of the camps, you know, I always need to know where the door is when I sleep."

As I waited for word about my surgery, I heard her story. My roommate was one of only 17 child survivors of Buchenwald. Her father had been murdered when she was five, and her mother was mostly absent, working as a doctor in the Red Army. After leaving the camps, a British patron had sent her to good schools in England, and eventually she came to Canada, where her young husband promptly left her with their two small sons. She got a job in a bank, became a stock trader, invested well in gold, and eventually was able to buy a house and a bit of land—enough to give away a few acres to a young mother in a similar plight. Then she earned a PhD, writing her thesis about the Depression and the 1929 crash.

I wondered why no one was phoning or visiting her. I was slightly skeptical of her saga. Where was her family? "My sons are working in Australia and the Antarctic now," she said, "but I don't want to call and get them worried."

The following night, one of the last things she told me through the curtain before we went to sleep was that she had also lost a three-year-old daughter to leukemia.

"Losing a child is the worst," she said softly. "That beats everything." Gwen couldn't read or watch TV, but had enough peripheral vision to get around. She lived alone, and preferred to. She seemed content.

I, on the other hand, had fallen off my bike on my way to a yoga class and would soon be Om-ing again.

Perspective is good.

I called Casey in Montreal and filled him in.

"Ouch," he said. "That's bad." We didn't discuss the fact that he was working as a bike courier in the downtown core of Montreal, a city not known for cautious drivers.

"Wear your helmet," I reminded him. "And don't swerve."

I came to enjoy Gwen's loquacious company. It seemed half the hospital knew and liked her too. And after unavoidably eavesdropping on her phone calls, I decided that her story was true and that she was the real thing: a survivor of the worst possible calamities—the Holocaust, and the loss of a child—who hadn't lost her kindness or optimism.

Late that night, they wheeled me down for surgery, which took place in the chilly bowels of the hospital, like something illegal. My surgeon was tall and patrician-looking, with blue eyes.

Maitre d'-ish. When I came out of the anesthetic, Brian was there, smiling at me, holding my hand. Not worried. Then it was back up to my room and Gwen.

The next night I felt an odd new pain in my back, under the left shoulder blade. Gwen was talking again, on the other side of the curtain. My lungs felt funny, raw. Finally, Gwen registered my silence and fell quiet. She sat on the edge of her bed, softly saying "oh dear" once in a while. Then she put on her yellow robe, inserted her injured foot into a giant surgical boot, and wheeled her walker out of the room. Going for a salubrious amble down the hall, I guessed. I was glad for the silence.

Much later, Gwen rolled back in with two large teas and a bag of cranberry scones on her walker tray. This had required a long, long journey from our Dickensian ward to another wing of the hospital, on another floor.

"I thought we needed a bit of change," she said, popping the lids off the teas.

There are times when a good cup of tea is the best possible medicine. As we sat eating our scones, a breathless man in a uniform dashed into the room. "Oh you made it, thank God!" he said to Gwen. He was a worker from the Second Cup who had seen her set off at an odd angle, bumping into walls, and worried that she might not make it back safely.

So many Samaritans. All kinder to me than my own thoughts.

The next day, I took a walk down the hall and felt short of breath. Well, I've just had surgery, I thought. But when two friends came to drive me home from the hospital, I couldn't manage the three blocks to their car.

"I'll just wait here," I said, hanging onto a fence. Back home, I settled in on the couch. My right arm was in a plaster cast and a sling. The hand sticking out of it was glossy and bluish, but the fingers worked. I could still type. I'll be back in action soon, I thought.

■

In the year of broken things, Casey had stayed on in Montreal to continue his graduate studies in Tortured Romance. The on-and-offness with Rebecca was now heading into its second winter. After graduating, he had set up a new apartment in untrendy Park Extension, on a street of Armenian and African and East Indian immigrants. It was a bright, cheap place with front and back balconies, across from a minuscule park. We gave him our shredded old leather couch and other bits of furniture. His best friend and roommate would be moving in when he got back from Japan. Casey advertised for a third person to share the apartment and a pixieish young woman responded. An aspiring writer, she lined her exotic teas up on the counter and seemed like the perfect fit.

In the meantime, every weekday morning, Casey biked off to his job in the rigging department of a company that supplied sound and light equipment for big stage events or concerts by Celine Dion and Springsteen when they came through town.

"It's the kind of job people take because they think it will make them part of show business," Casey noted wryly, including himself in this category.

He liked the physical side of the job—the lifting and lugging, and the camaraderie too. As the only Anglo in the Francophone company, he got to brush up on his *joual* and learn the finer points of wasting company time. Then on many evenings he would bike from work to Rebecca's apartment for more late-night wrestling with the relationship. I didn't hear the details, but I heard the exhaustion in his voice. They'd make new rules about spending time apart or texting.

Then break them.

When I got home from the hospital, the flow of soups, flowers, and good wishes began. Fractures are so unambiguous, I thought; if only anxiety required a plaster cast or a head halo. I was beginning to enjoy my invalid status, but the strange pain in my back was still there. As a well-read hypochondriac, I knew about the risk of blood clots after surgery and their potentially fatal journey through the lungs and into the heart or brain. But as usual, I decided I was over-thinking matters.

Still, when some friends arrived with dinner, I could scarcely sit at the table with them. I was very weak. My lungs ached. I was even more anxious than usual, if such a thing was possible.

I hobbled to the laptop to Google "embolisms." Intriguingly, anxiety is listed as an official symptom—the body sounding the alarm. It was a Saturday, of course. I phoned my doctor's office, and the physician on call got back to me.

"Well, I tend to tell anyone with shortness of breath after surgery to go to Emerg, just to be on the safe side," she said.

"But I feel too bad to go to the hospital," I whined. I'd had had enough of ER and waiting rooms.

The next morning, Brian drove me to my doctor. Walking up to her office felt like being at 26,000 feet. I dissolved in tears as I described my symptoms. Take her across the street to the hospital, she said.

"Might as well check this out," I said to Brian, sending him back to work to meet his deadline. "It's probably just post-traumatic crap. I'll phone you when I'm done."

An hour later I was having dye injected into my veins for a test revealing that I had two "rather large" pulmonary embolisms, one in each lung. The demeanour of the ER nurses subtly changed. They didn't meet my eye. The pace of things picked up. Someone came in and stuck a cartoonishly long needle in my stomach (Heparin, a clot buster). A young resident appeared with a clipboard and told me what to expect: home care, Heparin injections for a week, plus a regime of Coumadin, a blood thinner and former rat poison, to prevent new clots from forming. I would need weekly tests to measure the clotting rate of my blood and the level of Coumadin required. Too much of the drug caused internal bleeding (the secret to killing rats). Many people, I learned, take this drug every day.

And what happens to the clots in my lungs, I asked. I almost thought of them as pets. Or rats.

They will resolve on their own, in time.

Resolve, dissolve? How long does that take?

It depends. A few weeks or a couple months.

So this is serious, I said wonderingly, trying to catch up. The doctor was leaning against a gurney, hands folded over his clipboard.

Oh very serious, he said, with a slight air of chagrin.

"You could die," he said. "But that usually happens within the first hour." He looked at his watch.

My first thought, apart from dull alarm, was that I hadn't been overreacting to my symptoms after all. A lesson: honour your instincts.

They wanted to keep me in ER overnight, to "monitor things." I was in Women's College Hospital, where the ER is small and curiously peaceful. I had my own curtained cubicle. The doctor left. I sat on the edge of my gurney, by myself, and thought about whether I was ready to die.

I went down the list: my robust and youthful husband would miss me, but survive (if not move on to an immature, demanding, over-talkative trophy wife. Then he'd *really* miss me . . .). And despite his current dilemmas, I realized that my son was resourceful, strong, and on his way. In fact, the world would spin on quite nicely without me. Perhaps . . . my sense of being indispensable to everyone was up for revision?

Then I scanned my conscience; there were a few shadowy corners in the old hard drive but nothing to panic about. When I called Brian at work with the news, I lowballed the implications of the diagnosis but suggested he get on over. I punched in Janet's number again—"It's a much smaller ER this time"—and made light of the situation. My arm's doing really well, I said, but there was a tiny, tiny possibility that I could also die in the next few hours, and so I needed something decent to read and a pair of slippers. I heard her voice quaver, and that's when mine did too.

I decided not to phone Casey just yet. He'd be at work anyway. I'd give it another day. Presuming I had one. (He later rebuked us for this decision.)

Then calmly, calmly, I looked at my life, and thought: okay. If necessary I could wrap it up right now.

■

160   That fall, tired of working nine-hour days for minimum wage, Casey had switched to bike couriering and driving for a French meals-on-wheels organization. Staying in various sorts of motion. We are, I keep forgetting, a family of cyclists, skiers, and restless people. The love trouble with its attendant angst continued.

Then, in February of the broken year, Brian racked up a bike accident himself. (I suspected a competitive element at first but he was sideswiped by a car.) This left him with a mild concussion that made him act weird for several days and caused his groin, where it had been impaled on his handlebars, to turn an awesome shade of eggplant. He had to take a cellphone photo of his purple genitals for insurance purposes, and for months this image kept randomly popping up in our slideshows.

As for me, the embolisms "resolved" but the fallout continued, with a case of shingles over Christmas followed by news from the dentist that I had also broken a small bone in my jaw during the accident. Well, that would explain the constant headaches. I had to keep taking Coumadin. I was convinced that it jacked up my anxiety, but my hard-assed hematologist claimed there were absolutely no side effects from Coumadin—apart from the risks of internal bleeding and fetal defects in pregnant women. What other side effects does a drug need to invite skepticism, I wondered.

All I know is that for nearly a year, I felt as if I was operating inside my own electrically charged enclosure. I expected blue sparks to leap from my fingers when people shook my hand. I realized that the post-traumatic fallout from the whole life-and-death drama could account for my anxiety, if not my entire personality. But I preferred to blame the drug.

Nevertheless, I functioned and cooked dinner. I drove to therapy and did yoga, drank red wine, called my son, saw my friends. Everything felt like a mild ordeal.

Brian's mother was also in and out of hospital that winter, with alarming collapses. I became a connoisseur of different emergency rooms around the city, the ones with the best triage nurses or the worst coin machines for snacks. I learned that being 91 doesn't make a bit of difference but "Shortness of breath" (SOB) as a presenting symptom will sometimes help you jump the queue.

■

Meanwhile, the hard times were piling up for Casey, in fiendish new ways. When his friend moved in with him, Casey said to him, half-jokingly, because there was a history of this, "There's only one rule in this household—no sleeping with the roommate." Not unreasonable, in a three-person situation.

Need I drag this out? *Of course* the friend slept with the pixieish new roommate. In a twinkling they fell in love and became inseparable, doing everything as a couple. No more bocce ball outings for the boys.

Casey was under no illusions that he was the perfect roommate, given the craziness he was going through. But the irony of coming home from one obsessive romance to watch another one unfold was not lost on him.

THE BROKEN YEAR

"It's like Dante's description of Purgatory," he said on the phone one day, revealing that he had in fact read some books at McGill. "The punishment fits the nature of the crime. You're doomed to witness your own behaviour, enacted in front of your eyes, over and over."

I did think that Casey should cut his friend some slack—the guy didn't mean to fall in love, and roommates aren't forever. But he was irked by the way men can let their friendships languish as soon as a girlfriend comes along to take care of all their emotional needs. Women do that too, as I recalled. Courtship will dominate the whole agenda, if you let it.

As winter deepened, the new couple went into domestic high gear. There were doilies for the drinks, discussions about the state of the bathtub, and much folding of tea towels. The two of them were in bed by 10 p.m.

"It's a glass coffee table," Casey would report to us, wearily, "you don't need a doily on a glass coffee table."

"I put so much into making this work," he complained. He'd found the flat, furnished it, supplied the roommate, and now he was eating his dinners most nights down the street at the Vietnamese café rather than being the third wheel.

Homes don't usually last at your age, I sometimes said. Or just thought.

He had tried hard to get his life up and running this first year after college. To get work and love and friends in place around him. Instead, everything had fallen apart.

■

That Christmas Rebecca finished school, and they agreed to finally let it go. She moved back to Toronto and her family, with a plan to travel and do volunteer work in Chile. Five thousand miles of separation might do the trick.

In the New Year, his roommates announced that they had found an apartment in Little Italy but they had to move right away, in two weeks. They felt badly about the whole situation and not giving more notice, especially since it was the middle of January. But the new place was really perfect.

Casey began scrolling through Craigslist again.

Spring

I'VE COME THROUGH MONTREAL by train. Things have finally settled down on the health front, and I'm going up to our summer cabin to get some concentrated work done. Brian will drive the car and catch up with me on the weekend. It's been a while since I've visited the city, and I'm curious to see Casey's new place.

The apartment is back in Mile End, a few blocks from where he used to live on Jeanne-Mance. A neighbourhood full of beautiful girls on bicycles. He's sharing with two women his age with messy bedrooms who have painted the kitchen a great shade of red. It's only a sublet, but that might change.

His new room is long and spacious, with blond wood floors and tall windows that open wide and have no screens. He demonstrates, standing on the ledge.

"Montrealers don't worry about suicide," he says merrily.

I haven't seen him since Christmas. He's been following a post-breakup health and sanity program—swimming, biking, working on various job proposals. He's got a contract doing some archiving for a film company downtown. It's heavy on the data-processing but leaves him lots of freedom.

He looks good, clear-eyed. New jeans, too, I notice, for the office. He has some money in the bank now and has bought a bottle of wine for my arrival, which we open.

A tour of his room: the main feature is an organized cockpit of turntable, amplifier, recording stuff, beside a clean desk. His headphones hang neatly from a nail in the wall.

"The whole thing about work, I've figured out, is appearances," he says. "When the job has no actual content, which mine currently doesn't, all that matters is that you look busy and dress appropriately."

Before I left Toronto, I had resorted to a diagnostic tool I don't often use these days. I consulted the I Ching. Very 1971 of me, I realize. And yes, it's a military-minded text with antique views on gender, but I've always found something useful in the readings. They tend to throw a fresh light on whatever is uppermost in my mind, regardless of what question I ask. Usually my question is "What's going on here?"

I tossed the coins six times and arrived at the 48th hexagram, The Well, with two "moving" lines. It's always good to get moving lines, because they offer more specific commentary and indicate change.

The reading described a situation where a communal well was under construction but couldn't be used until the town around it became more organized and the well was properly cared for. I read the text for the first moving line:

The well is cleaned, but no one drinks from it.
This is my heart's sorrow,
For one might draw from it.
If the king were clear-minded,
Good fortune might be enjoyed in common.

Then the second moving line:

*True, if a well is being lined with stone, it cannot be used while
the work is going on. But the work is not in vain; the result is
that the water stays clear.*

*In life also there are times when a man must put himself in
order. During such a time he can do nothing for others, but his
work is nonetheless valuable, because by enhancing his powers
and abilities through inner development, he can accomplish all
the more later on.*

■

I sit down at his desk and look out the window, through the rain
that is falling, at the grey stone apartments across the street and the
spring garbage on the wet lawns. The curl of the black balconies
down to the street, like diagrams of DNA. Montreal is so Montreal.
Ten frames of a movie and you can recognize that it was shot here.
Long ago Montreal imagined itself as bigger, more urban, more
ambitious, and the mood lingers on. One block over is Saint-
Urbain, Mordecai Richler's turf. All the fireworks of Brian's twenties
took place here, a few streets away. It's a city that asks to be written
about, that makes you feel as if you're in a story.

Casey calls up some of his music files on the computer and plays
me some of the tunes he has been recording.

"They're mostly quiet ones because I have to record them at
night when there are people around. I'll burn you a CD to take up
to the cottage," he says, pointing out the tall, handy stack of blanks.
He starts scrolling through his list, choosing recent songs of his
own. "I'm trying to sort out some of the more bitter ones," he jokes.

He plays one, a spooky late-night blues called "Blessing in Dis-
guise." About the bad taking you into the vicinity of something new
and good.

"Check this out," he says, switching to some whirling Turkish
numbers with an ululating female vocal. He turns and gives me one

of his wide, blazing smiles as we both listen to the woman sing, riding the crazy waves of the music like someone on a Jet Ski.

It is raining hard outside, but we put on our jackets and walk a few blocks over to find somewhere to eat. People are in the streets despite the weather. On the corner is an Indonesian restaurant with white tablecloths, its windows rectangles of warmth and light in the rain. We step inside.

Not My Job

I HAVE DONE IT AGAIN, overstepping my boundaries as a "helpful" mother to my job-hunting son. All with the best of intentions of course.

The problem with an arts degree—one of them, that is—is that unless you want to be an academic or a museum curator, you end up looking for work in a swampy field called "communications." These job descriptions are often written in something like Esperanto, a highly evolved form of gibberish that obscures the true nature of the job. "Office management" could mean six hours of photocopying a day and "excellent interpersonal skills" can be work-speak for "receptionist babe with a nice smile."

Until recently Casey had spurned this end of the work spectrum, preferring to live the non-cubicle life. Then he began applying for more professional positions.

Sometimes I'd troll through the jobsite listings myself, an unwise activity that can lead to "forwarding." These sites can also be slightly addictive, like taking online house tours. But it cheered me up to be able to contemplate careers other than freelance writing. I was sure that I could "participate in designing both print and digital design strategies" for someone. It wasn't too late, perhaps, for me to become a professional cake decorator.

One day he sent us the descriptions for a couple jobs he had applied for that sounded promising. Both were well-paying positions requiring years of experience in their respective fields. Neither was out of his league in terms of his skills ("communication" and writing) or strengths (working with people, managing projects). But in the past decade the etiquette of applying for a job has ramped up to a level where every detail matters, no matter how picayune. Did he know this?

Only 24 hours earlier, when I was bugging him about a barista gig he didn't even want, he had asked me to lay off with the job advice. But I couldn't restrain myself; I didn't want him to waste his time collecting no's. During my stints as a magazine editor, I've been on the receiving end of pitches, queries, and cover letters. I knew how quickly one misspelling can land someone on the rejection pile.

So I sent him an email with a few carefully chosen suggestions regarding the art of résumés and cover letters.

This did not go over well.

He did not require redundant professional advice, he informed me, and indeed he found it "fundamentally insulting." Everything I advised him on, he already knew, thank you very much. He had already talked to a career counsellor at McGill. He understood cover letters. Yes, he tailored his CV to each different position. THIS IS NOT YOUR JOB, he emailed in caps. And if I wanted him to continue to take my advice seriously, I should consider not giving it unless asked for.

Gulp.

I phoned him, apologized, and said I would try harder on the not-meddling front. The air was cleared. But I knew my impulse to "help" would swing back again. I tend to be meddling and entrepreneurial with most of my friends, so it's difficult to censor this impulse with my own son.

This is the stress of motherhood at the twenty-something, middle-management stage, when you are confronted with a problem (your son is looking for a job) without having any agency or power in the situation (you are no longer the boss). Much of the necessary un-mothering that goes on with grown-up kids falls into this category, where the main challenge is to shut up and go along with other people's decisions, good or bad. Breathing exercises also help.

And it's not the case that I always leap in unbidden; our son does ask for guidance from us at times, or at least a sympathetic ear. When things get discouraging on the job-hunting front—hard to avoid, given the current unemployment rates among the young, which are twice as high as adult figures—my natural response is: how can we fix this? What practical advice can I offer? I want the world to make use of all the things he has to offer. Instead, my advice can come across as a lack of faith in his abilities to make his own way.

Doing stuff for him as a child always came easily: the costume-making, hamster-feeding, chauffeuring parts. Being that kind of mother felt like a holiday from other responsibilities. But this category of help is tougher: *not* doing things for him. Mothers of grown kids must learn new tricks of the lip-zipping sort. Empathetic listening, responding in short sentences, preferably while making a large vat of bean soup. "That must be tough" is okay, and "We'll keep our fingers crossed" is too. "You might think about a haircut before that interview" is not acceptable.

Then I would remind myself that my son was only a year out of school and still learning the ropes. "Putting on his game face," as he said. I've been officially employed for perhaps a total of five years out of the past 40 so I am hardly in a position to tutor him in the ways of the "real world." But I still have to remind myself that my urge to edit, to make sure that all the commas and dashes are in place, should not be transferred to my son, his haircuts, or his life.

And when I was in my twenties, as I recall, I committed some professional faux pas that still give me pain.

■

I was freelancing for the *Toronto Star*, writing entertainment listings (but with a Proustian flair, I thought). I had worked myself into a froth of indignation about the fact that my editors had failed to offer me a column of my own in the newspaper. The thing reporters work decades to earn normally. Hadn't they noticed the wit and nuance of my listings for fall fairs and outdoor concerts? How long did they expect me to toil in these menial assignments?

But I didn't have the nerve to speak to my editor or to do something professional, such as submitting a column on spec. Instead, I wrote a chippy little note about how my talents were far better suited to a column and how could this be redressed? Then, even more bizarrely, I tucked this note into the open purse of my editor, on her desk.

We never spoke of it. I never brought it up, and neither did she because she was a kind woman. Luckily, she didn't fire me.

It was also at the *Star* that I spent a few months pinch-hitting for the book editor, who was on leave. I enjoyed the work but it came with a windowless office under fluorescent lights. Unacceptable! I was an outdoorsy girl and simply couldn't function without daylight, even though I should have been grateful I wasn't out there toiling in the newsroom with everyone else. When it came time to hire a new book editor, they gave me the courtesy of an interview.

I breezed in and began kibitzing with the interviewing editor. "Just two things," I said, "there's no way I can work in a windowless office, and I wouldn't consider any salary under. . . ." And I named a ridiculous figure, I think it might have been $18,000 a year. This was 1975, remember. An arts position. The lips of the editor across from me twitched as he suppressed a smile. "Well, the salary starts at $24,000," he said.

I was also fired from one of my first jobs, as an editorial assistant for a small publishing house. I thought I was doing fine, writing long, intensely articulate letters of rejection to the authors in the slush pile. But there were money issues and some office politics; the easiest resolution was to eliminate my job. The editor who hired me was kind about breaking the news. Unfortunately, I was inexperienced in being fired and I didn't know that when this takes place you are *not supposed to show up* the next morning. I thought it would show character to work the following day to wrap up the projects on my desk.

I was sitting there dutifully typing when the editor came into the small office we shared.

"What are you doing here?" he said, possibly worried that I might never leave. No. It was just that I didn't understand the etiquette of being fired.

Being hired has its unwritten rules too. Which my son has figured out. At 27 he is more job savvy than I ever was.

■

In studies of workplace satisfaction, the bottom line isn't the size of the salary or the amount of responsibility you wield. It's the sense of agency and being able to measure your impact on a project. When the job at hand is motherhood and the project is "assisting" your son as he looks for employment, sometimes the best strategy is the most unsatisfying one—to lay down tools.

Or enlist his father. Boys want more guidance from their fathers anyway. And way less from their mind-reading mothers.

The Other Shoe

"Sometimes I think our whole family should just shut up."
— Casey Johnson

O UR SON and a friend, Adrienne, were on their way to spend a few days with us at the cottage. It was mid-August, and the days were getting shorter. After dark, when they were late to arrive, I headed down the gravel road to the sweet spot where I can usually get cellphone reception. I was going to call him to make sure all was well.

The "cottage" is a small cabin in the Laurentians we've been renting for the past 10 years. There's no one else on the crescent-shaped lake except for us and the owners of the property, Anne and Arne, who live down the road with their two kids, Sara and Daniel. The lake sits on top of a hill, once volcanic, and backs onto miles of forest reserve land. Over the years the owners have become friends, and during his Montreal years Casey would spend the odd restorative weekend with them, chopping wood and hanging out with a family who do stuff without writing about it.

This is where Brian and I spend our summer holidays and relax. Casey loves the place too. But when all three of us are there, in the one small cabin with a spare bed in the loft, there's no escaping family tensions. Sometimes this is where they get played out.

Last year Brian and Casey had their showdown, talking for hours at the end of the dock. I felt a bit guilty that I got off scot-free. But the next summer, the other shoe dropped.

■

On the road I saw the approach of his car headlights and scampered back toward the cabin, embarrassed to be caught punching away at my phone. I saw by how he braked and jumped out of the car that my anxiety had already, in two seconds, annoyed him.

"Were you planning to meet me on the highway?"

"I was just coming out here to call," I said sheepishly. Then we went inside, where he regaled us with stories of the grand old Laurentian cottage he and his friends had just visited. He was full of energy, having just swum three kilometres down their lake and played a game of tennis. Now he was under our tiny roof again. I watched him from a distance, hoping this extroverted shine wouldn't wear off under our parental gaze.

A few weeks earlier, I had sent him one too many messages about some music website I thought he might be interested in. (Attempts at hip mothering are generally a bad idea.) I had the feeling that this summer the time had come for my smiting. Everything I said and did lately seemed to rub him the wrong way.

■

The next morning, Anne and Arne and their kids were going for a walk, on a new trail they'd made through the woods, to the cliffs. It was early (my version of early), I hadn't eaten breakfast, and wasn't up for a trek.

"I'll catch up," I said half-heartedly.

"I doubt it," Casey said. Not that he cared that much if I came along; it was the bullshit factor that bothered him.

Everyone headed off into the woods.

I ate some toast, put on my trail shoes, and ran through the wet grass, trying to catch up to the group to show him that his mother was a better person than he thought. I went the wrong way up the trail, but it was good to be on the move. At the top of the cliffs, I stopped for the never-disappointing view of the dark blue mountains to the north. Then I heard the snap of branches. Their son Daniel on his mountain bike thundered by, followed by the dog, everyone else, and Casey.

"You see," said Anne, when she saw me coming toward them, "she did make it after all."

"Was Casey disparaging me?" I said jovially.

"Yes, he was; he said you'd never catch up."

"But I did," I said, falling into step behind Anne.

Brian was the only one missing; he was eating a leisurely breakfast back at the cabin, free of ambivalence or guilt about such outings.

That weekend Casey was looking at us through son-goggles and seeing wall-to-wall neuroses. It's true, the older you get, the more gargoylish all your mannerisms become. Just the way we both get into the lake: either standing thigh-high in the water for a very long time while waving the arms before pushing off (me) or standing on the dock, peering up at the clouds, waiting for a "window of sun" to dive in (Brian). It reminded me of a habit my father had; he would come through the front door and fall to his knees to pluck lint off the rug. More fodder for amusing stories about my family, for friends. Just as our habits are for Casey. But it also hurts when your own warm son starts viewing you through the other end of the binoculars.

It had been a frustrating year for him. He had worked on several ambitious proposals that had disappeared into the ether. I didn't help matters when I tried to talk him into an internship with an institution that had already turned one project of his down. I was trying to make the point that you have to be persistent and not take rejections too personally.

This is advice I have never been able to accept myself.

Nevertheless, I pressed on. I talked, Adrienne knitted.

"Remember how your mother always saved your high-school textbooks in case you became a teacher instead of a writer?" Casey said, scowling at me as he lay on the too-short couch in our cabin. "How it really annoyed you? So, don't do that. Don't keep giving me belligerent advice about what I should do with my life. It's all kinda tenuous right now, everything I'm doing, and I don't really need the extra pressure of you saying, 'Have you thought about broadcasting college?'"

Later in the day, he went for a long swim and then lay on the dock. I was sitting near him in a white plastic chair, with a book in my lap, not quite reading. The mergansers swam by, leaving little V's behind them.

"It's probably delusional," Casey mused, "but I wouldn't mind being a pilot. Or maybe a bush pilot."

I did not cite grim statistics about the dangers of bush piloting. I did not point out the years of tedious training required.

"That could work," I said.

Everything was up in the air for him that weekend: his Montreal sublet was about to end, and the prospects for work in that city's Anglo marketplace were not looking good. At the kitchen table, he sat at the laptop scrolling through Craigslist. Then out of the blue an email arrived from a friend in Toronto who had a room to rent, right away.

Moving to Toronto would mean more job possibilities and the company of old friends. He'd be closer to home, which might or might not be a plus. But it would require turning another new page in an already turbulent year.

"When does she need to know?" I asked.

"By Tuesday." Two days.

"So go down and check out what's available in Montreal, then make a decision, call her."

A frown. "I'm not sure I want to pull up stakes so quickly in Montreal."

"But it's perfect, the apartment's in a great location."

"The rent's $650."

"That's nothing for Toronto."

More frowning.

"I'm trying to be more patient about making sure I make decent decisions, rather than barking up the wrong trees."

"Well, that makes sense."

I shut up. Hung the towels up and straightened the books on the side table, took the bananas off the window sill so they won't go all black and mushy (again).

Then I went on about the internship one more time.

"Don't reject it out of hand," I said, "just because a woman in another department said no to something else."

He looked impatient.

"Lots of people apply over and over, and sometimes persistence pays off."

Adrienne, a visual artist who works at a library, was still knitting and enduring our conversation.

"I applied 14 times for my job," she chimed in, "and eventually I got it."

I could see that Casey was getting angry but I persisted. I didn't just want to be blandly supportive for the sake of keeping the peace. I thought that although he had been more than diligent about applying for jobs, he needed to make some plans, soon, for the coming year. And if he didn't have any, then I would push a couple on him, even at the risk of upsetting him.

"I don't want you to be reflexively negative about things you haven't tried yet," I said. "Why can't you be more receptive to things? I have some good ideas."

"Yes, but you think your ideas are better than my ideas."

"No, I don't."

"Yes, you do."

"Well, some of my ideas *are* good."

Although it was chilly and the wind was picking up, he went down to the dock, stood in the water for a time, and then pushed off, doing his strong, measured crawl to the middle of the lake. He had taken to doing marathon swims, sometimes an hour long, to help purge the frustrations of being in limbo and being with his family.

This was new. I could feel a complete rejection of me and my every opinion radiating off him. It was necessary and understandable, him not wanting to fall back into the embrace of the family. And I *was* being relentless. But I still found it bruising. I felt silly and crone-ish. I remembered my own grandmother, when I was four years old, flapping her apron and saying, "Take care! Take care!" as I slid down the banister. Now I was her.

Unspoken anger filled the cabin. I sat in the new glider-rocker I had just found at a yard sale, autistically rocking back and forth, unable to concentrate on anything. Casey lay on the couch, apologizing for being edgy but still edgy. With an arm over his brow, he tried to sleep. Adrienne knitted. Brian retreated to the bedroom, where his computer was set up. Dusk arrived. I felt mortified and sad.

I wanted to grab him by the shoulders and propel him down to the dock, look up at the stars, and say, "You have made me angry too. You're stubborn and you think all my advice is stupid. But it's not, and when you continue to not know where you are headed, it's hard not to rush in with our suggestions."

The night of our argument, I went to bed angry and fed up. Fine then, I thought pettishly, blow off the support and helpful perks of your parents. Make your own way, stay out in the rain. I lay with my head burning on the pillow, vowing to never send him a helpful email again.

180

And for once, I stopped worrying. His life was his problem. Good luck to him.

■

The next day when I was on the porch, he came out and sat beside me. I apologized and promised (again, but with new resolve) to stop with the work advice. He said he was sorry for being so touchy. He didn't need to add that this had come at the end of a lousy year for him, during which he had worked hard for little money and had been ill for weeks on end.

I remembered my post-graduation year of panic attacks in banks and subways, the same year I was dumped by my first big love, then quickly fired from my second job. I realized that this is just part of the story of your twenties, but it was tough to see my son going through it too.

Anne and Arne were scheduled to do a roofing job on another cottage the following day and they asked Casey if he felt like giving them a hand. Working at something as opposed to thinking about everything seemed like a good idea, so he agreed. Brian and I were not disappointed at the prospect of having the lake to ourselves for the day.

Every summer, in August, there are usually one or two afternoons that feel unusually still. You can sense summer turning on its axis. One or two flares of red leaves begin to show up among the trees around the shoreline. These windless, hot days feel like a gathering before the season tips toward fall.

Brian and I spent most of the day on the dock, covered up with hats and towels under a clear sky and an intense sun. I thought about them working on the roof, in this heat. I was glad not to be there. We went up to the shade of the cottage in the afternoon and took advantage of our privacy.

Late, around 8 p.m., the car came up the road and dropped Casey off. He looked pale and complained of nausea and a headache. They had decided to keep on working and finish the job in one day, but it was hellishly hot on the roof, and he had sunstroke. Or heat exhaustion, or heat stroke—I knew the differences among those three were important, but I couldn't remember what they were.

Casey went up to the loft and lay down. His face and neck were flushed but his skin was dry and clammy. Ever since Mexico, his tolerance for heat had diminished. I gave him lots of water, and then Brian and I walked up the road to have dinner with the others.

During dessert we got a text from Casey, but it didn't make any sense: "Not feeling . . ." something something. I walked back down to our cabin. He was lying up in the dark, a bit deranged and delirious, his skin fiery to the touch. "I'm not feeling top-notch" was what he had tried to text.

I got some cold towels and put them on his head. I thought about where the nearest hospital was and whether we owned a thermometer. I was back in that familiar place, the calm, alert, mom-on-call place.

There's an extra mattress in the loft, so I slept on that, a few feet away from Casey. I checked his forehead during the night. His skin blazed away but didn't sweat. Sometimes he woke up, and I would give him water, and he'd drop back into sleep. He seemed grateful I was there. At a certain point, around dawn, his body began to cool down again.

The next morning, three hummingbirds began to trisect the air like lasers, zooming in on the feeder that hangs outside our window, then darting away. Hum, hover, sip, retreat. I borrowed Arne's long tree clipper to prune away some of the ferns and foliage that were coming between us and the lake. Casey slowly made his way down the loft staircase, and said he thought he might be able to eat something. The heat spell had passed.

■

During the day, we played Scrabble (Brian won, as usual). Casey tried to get certain "Japanese" words by us. Because CBC radio features prominently at the cottage, we made up a song about the new morning host, trying to find all the rhymes for "Ghomeshi" ("He's no Joe Pesci . . .") and recorded it on the laptop. It sounded pretty good. We got our laughter back.

Casey came up with an idea for a movie that would require everyone in the audience to wear sunglasses. He worked on the story while I took notes. "What's at stake for the characters?" Brian reminded us. "There has to be something at stake." We went back and forth, developing the plot, getting excited about it. Then came a swimming break, after which I made a peach crumble. At dusk, invisible bugs began to pucker the surface of the lake. One fish jumped, a sudden silver flash.

183

"Don't forget to send me a copy of those notes," Casey said before he climbed the ladder to the loft.

26 and 99

MY 99-year-old mother is dying. No one could argue that this is surprising or wrong, but I doubt that her age will subtract from the fact of her death. The flame of life either burns in someone or it has gone out, and one moment can't be confused with the other. I told myself that this wasn't anything to make a big fuss about and that dying will be a relief for her. But of course, it's your one and only mother who is vanishing. There's no getting around that.

She's been in long-term care now for almost three years, most of that time immobilized in a wheelchair as her vision continues to fade. Her great intelligence remains, but the focus of it often wavers and blurs. Sometimes she is confused and calls me her sister; sometimes she tells us that her long-dead father came to visit and hung the painting of flowers above her bed. Other times she is on the ball, caustic and more searingly honest than anyone else in the room.

I'm thinking she will die at any minute. But although she is profoundly weak, barely able to push the words out when she tries to talk, she keeps taking another breath. The body just wants to go on living, the way a dog wants to run. Her physical presence in the bed, even though she scarcely moves, is still powerful, almost radiant, like Precambrian rock under tremendous pressure. The glossy cheekbones stand out, the eye sockets are deeper, a rosy colour, and her face, strangely unlined, looks carved and iconic. "Like a face on a totem pole," Casey said after one visit.

When her eyes open, they stare straight ahead, far away, until I step into the path of her vision, and she finds me.

"Is that you?"

"Yes. It's Marni."

"I was just sleeping."

"Yes. You don't have to wake up, I can just sit here and keep you company."

She draws in a sigh. Even that is too much work.

"You'll be bored here." A mutter.

"No, I won't. I like seeing you. I can just sit here and read while you sleep."

She is talking again, but the words are too soft and garbled. I come closer and lean over her.

"Do you have a good book?" she asks.

"It's okay. It's about divorce."

"Oh, that's terrible."

"Well, you don't need to read it. Not after 68 years of marriage."

"And nothing to show for it."

"Don't be ridiculous." Once again, I enumerate all her accomplishments, her artistic talent, her beautiful house, her three children, her three grandchildren, her great-grandson. Then I say, "And they all have a great love for you." It's my sensitive bedside manner, running away with me.

She says something I can't hear. I lean over her again.

"I can't imagine," she says, "having a great love for anyone."

Well, that's consoling, I think. But I know it's just her radar picking up on my slightly phony "deathbed" vocabulary. The editor in her, weakened but still potent.

"Maybe you do, though. You love your children greatly, don't you?"

"Oh yes," she says ardently, remembering.

"Well, that's how we feel about you."

Her eyes close. Her skin is papery white, and her face is riveting. A week ago her cheek felt too warm, but now it feels too cool, deserted by the blood. She falls back into sleep, her diaphragm working to pull in air. I sit in my chair and read my book, a review assignment. Every few pages I look over to make sure the blankets still rise and fall.

Her feet under the sheets are shrouded in down booties. There is a pressure sore on her back, and she must be turned every two hours. She doesn't complain and mostly saves her energy to utter the necessary commands: put me flat, turn down the light, I'd like a drink. She doesn't look happy, but I tell myself that this might just be muscular, a stiffening of the face. I wish the woman in the room next door would turn down her TV, a moronic throb that comes through the wall and must colour my mother's dreams. Fury wells up in me, an amorphous anger that has found a convenient target.

■

The next time I visit my mother, Casey comes with me.

He has no qualms about the deathbed, although once, after a visit, he said the experience was more exhausting than running 15 kilometres. It's the vampire effect, the hunger of the old for his youth. When he walks through the common room of the facility, where the crooked, the tremulous, and the silent are lined up in wheelchairs, the energy seems to come off him in waves; the old feast on him with their eyes. Sometimes they reflexively reach a hand out to him. "Hello," he says to Mabel, the one with the bemused smile who is always bent over, investigating her own feet. "Hey there, how's it going?" he says to the thin woman who prowls the corridors in her blue slippers and meets your gaze conspiratorially. Then he walks into his grandmother's room and pulls a chair up close to her.

"Hi Grandma, it's Casey." Her eyes open in their thousand-yard stare and then slowly, swimmingly, focus on him. Her mouth shapes words. We lean in.

"Handsome as ever," she manages. Repartee, the last thing to go.

"How're you doing, Grandma?" A rhetorical question. He takes her hands, which are puffy, in his.

"Oh, not too good."

"That's okay. You've done a lot in your life; you can take it easy now."

"I think I could walk," she says "but they don't want me to." An old refrain. She still plans to walk, even though it's been two years since she has taken a step.

Casey holds her hand while I putter around the room, watering the dying African violet, eating a stale chocolate out of the box on her dresser, cranking open the window to get some air into the stuffy room. Now it's as if visitors distract her from the strenuous work of crossing over to new terrain. The process of dying, if it isn't abrupt, takes longer than you expect. It runs by a different clock. Every time I see her, she has moved a notch farther away from us. I almost hesitate to call her back into the room, with us.

Furtively, when I'm alone with her, I tell her she can do as she likes now, that we're all fine, and she's free to go. She doesn't answer. Or she might say, "Well, if you have pills, you could give them to me." "Medicine, you mean?" "No, not medicine," she says firmly. But I don't have those pills and I don't think I could do it anyway.

Then she will ask me if "our" mother is still alive. She worries about her mother and seems to miss her, like a child. I imagine I'll be the same when I'm 99.

When she murmurs something about us "beating the traffic," it's a sign that we should go. But I like being in the room with her when she's asleep; it's comforting. The last time I visited, I stayed on for an hour or so. Then I crept over, because I couldn't see the blankets moving any more and I got alarmed. I was staring at her belly, waiting for it to rise, when her eyes sprang opened.

"What are you doing?" my mother asked.

"Uh, just looking at you." She looked skeptical. At least I didn't hold a mirror up to her mouth.

Later, in the car, Casey and I talked about what it's like to be in the presence of dying. "There's so much going on," he marvelled. "Sitting beside her, it's like sitting beside the ocean. It's intense."

"It was a good time to visit," I said, and then we let the radio play.

■

Back in the room, we give her some water, a thickened syrup of 189 water that won't cause her to choke, and a few spoonfuls of apple-sauce. But eating looks like something that makes no sense to her any more, and soon she says, "Enough."

Casey asks if she's tired.

"I think if you leave and I leave, then it will be best for both of us," she says. Gentle. I feel the effort it takes for her to deal with us, so casually alive.

"I'll see you soon," Casey says with a smile, "I love you very much, Grandma." My mother looks at him frankly. Even though she's not in the habit of making such statements, she rallies.

"I love you too."

"Sweet dreams," he says.

But she's already falling back into the new place, where it's easiest to float now.

As we gather up our things to leave, I turn the lights down, pull the blankets up to her neck. Tuck her in. The emergency call button is pinned to her pillow, but she's too weak to push it now. Or wouldn't. I tell her I'll see her tomorrow and pull the door half shut.

Casey lopes through the common room, past the other residents, trailing his youth and energy like a comet's tail.

Hello, Goodbye

I T'S LATE AUGUST. I'm 63, with a metal plate in my right elbow and too old to be helping my grown son move. He has it all organized, with friends at this end. But here I am anyway, wearing age-inappropriate capris, standing on College Street at Shaw, the Toronto equivalent of his old neighbourhood in Montreal. I peer east up into the river of rush-hour traffic as I wait for Casey to arrive in a U-Haul with all his earthly goods. He is moving back to the city, but not, to our mutual relief, into his old room. As he cheerfully said, a propos of living under the same roof with us, "Nothing personal, but it's unsustainable."

Seven years earlier, he had to go all the way to Guatemala to draw the line. Now he just needs to be on the other side of town. This seems to be what families keep on doing. We pull away from each other then pick up the phone.

It felt like the right time to move. If you're not in college, in love, or playing in a band named Border Collie, Montreal can be, as Casey put it, "a cruel mistress." Not the easiest place to find work or to put down roots. In the six years he lived there, he had come to know the far corners of the city intimately. He'd consumed a thousand warm bagels on St. Viateur and shared a huge loft in the east end with some bohemian yoga girls. He'd worked six jobs, climbed Mount Royal countless times, and played some Hank Williams at The Wheel Club. But now the city wasn't returning his calls.

In an email, he described to us his last summer weekend in the city, when he rode his bike around some of his old haunts. There was an outdoor tango festival in Parc Lafontaine. He sat on the grass and watched the couples dance, the city's haughty kiss good-bye. Last tango in Montreal. He threw a desultory farewell party, and his former roommates showed up. But that was bittersweet too.

"The city seems emptied of all my hopes and dreams now, and looks completely different," he wrote, well aware of how melodramatic that sounded. It's only a five-hour train ride from Toronto, not Kazakhstan, I thought. But I understood the logic; he was doing his best to make this the end of a certain chapter in his life, so that a new one could begin.

■

My cell rings. It's Casey, saying that he's a few blocks away. It's not six o'clock yet; he's early, but that's good because it means he can still park legally in front of the apartment to unload. I step off the curb to claim the spot. The apartment he's moving into is up one flight up, above Super Models Pizza ("Our crusts are thin as a supermodel").

Early in the day, he had phoned from the wheel of the U-Haul, on the 401, to report that a SUV had just pulled by him hauling a huge sailboat. The boat had fishtailed wildly, swerved, and then rolled off the road right in front of Casey.

"I knew when he passed me that he was trouble, so I made sure to put some distance between us," he said. The SUV driver was parked on the shoulder, waiting for the police to show up. Casey was behind him, ready to nose back into the stream of traffic. He sounded calm. It seemed to take the nervous edge off the journey, that little brush with bad luck.

A few days earlier, I had come by the apartment to pick up the keys. The place was bright but airless and hot. Katie said that it became even more stifling when the pizza ovens were all firing down below them. "The girl who rented it before us said 'the apartment really holds the heat,'" she said, "and I thought that would be a good thing in the winter."

Katie's partner Alex, an old friend of Casey's, had been accepted for an internship in another city, so she was glad to be able to have someone to share the rent with for the next few months. It would give him time to scout his own place. She showed me his tiny room, her former office, noting that it had no closet. "So I guess he'll do the boy thing," she said, meaning stacks of milk crates. But fresh pizza would not be a problem.

Now we would be living at opposite ends of College, the street that runs across the middle of Toronto from High Park and Little Italy to Cabbagetown. The red and yellow streetcars, which always make me think of an embolism shunting through the veins of the city, would pass right under his window.

Before, whenever he came home from Montreal to visit, he would occupy the spare room next to our bedroom. When everyone was in their rooms all we had to do was raise our voices to carry on a conversation. Life at the summer cabin was the same; we seem to gravitate toward small, yurt-like dwellings where we all live in the smoke of our cooking and the damp footprints of trips to the shower and back. It's partly economics, but perhaps a relic of our communal days, too—or of life in a band's touring van (that never goes anywhere).

Living under one roof, though, it's hard for a 23-year-old not to see himself constantly reflected in the funhouse mirror of his parents, with his image either magnified or distorted. The maternal reflexes keep twitching away too. My compulsion to put a vitamin pill beside his cereal or to dig out warmer scarves.

After a certain point, living together makes everyone feel trapped in dusty roles. To have him in the same city but not down the hall felt just right. Not just home, but a hometown.

Six-fifteen. A few blocks east, in the shining flow of metal I spot a white truck—surely too big a container for his bicycles, guitar cases, and Ikea bed. But I can see that it is Casey at the wheel. He pulls up to the curb, careful not to hit the parking meter with the truck's wide mirrors, and jumps out. Heat comes off the engine in waves.

"Look," he says, pointing at the inch between the tire walls and the curb. "Now, that's parking."

He's wearing cut-off jeans and a sleeveless black T-shirt, with a big smile on his face. He loves driving a truck. Just then his friend Tom shows up to help him unload. He doesn't need my help but he's appreciative of the welcome. Brian calls to say he's on his way over from the office on his bike. I peer into Super Models Pizza with what I hope is a friendly wave and pick up whatever lamps and baskets I can carry with my re-engineered elbow.

The men run up and down with bed frames and 50-pound amps. Soon I've done the small bits and stand around on the sidewalk feeling redundant. This becomes our last parental chore—to dwindle, to clam up, to say, "Well, you may be right," and step aside. Once we eclipsed everything, bending over their cribs. We were the whole sky. But eventually, at 16 or 26, they realize that whenever we come in to cover them up, we also block their view.

On the other hand, I did leave the gym early in order to show up at the apartment in good time. Katie was away for the weekend, so I'd opened the windows in the apartment, moved the mail off the stairs, and put some flowers in a vase. Bought some milk and put it in the fridge. That wasn't meddling, was it, to buy some milk? The thoughtful gesture of one adult to another?

Brian arrived breathless and clapped Casey on the back. "Your first Toronto apartment," he said. "This is a landmark!"

Up and down we went with bins of clothing, camping gear, my father's old record turntable, crates of our vinyl albums. Bikes and canvases. Casey gave me back the lamp I had ordered online for Seasonal Affective Disorder.

"I appreciate the gesture," he said, "but I don't plan on being depressed this winter."

No problem, I said. I know lots of depressed people who could use it.

His small room quickly filled up. The overflow went into a porch-like storage space at the back of the apartment.

"You know," I said to Casey, "you should just keep your bed in the room and put everything else back in that space—you could even put up shelves there for your clothes."

"Sounds like a plan," he said, as in, "I'm going to ignore that."

Stealthily, I lugged some crates from the bedroom back into the space. I began to organize a "music corner" at one end, a "tool and equipment corner" in another. *Stop it, stop it.* I slid open the windows for more air and looked down into the jumbled yard. Yes, this place had potential. I happened to have brought along a plate of jerk chicken so I put that in the fridge too.

"Will you be eating here or somewhere else?" I asked.

"I've got to drop off more stuff to another address, then I think I'll come home to sleep because it'll be too late to get myself set up here."

Home? Here, or back with us? The meaning of the word was shifting.

Then he barrelled off to deliver a mattress to someone in north Toronto, a moving job to help defray the cost of the truck. Brian got back on his bike; I carried the Saran-wrapped plate of chicken back to our car and drove home, where the two of us would eat it. The centrifugal household.

I felt fully in the ambiguous grip of family, this long-term arrangement in which the connection feels either too attenuated or too claustrophobic. It's also a lot for three people to sustain, architecturally speaking. We'd come through shaky times but here we were, still standing. How hard we make our children work, to absorb all our love, fears, and hopes.

What we could really use, I thought, was some new weight-bearing members . . . a daughter-in-law. Grandchildren. The wider circle.

The Dump

T HE MOVING-DAY adrenalin was still flowing, and Casey had one more day left on the rental fee of the truck.

"Maybe we should clear some of that stuff out of the basement."

Ah, the basement. The lurking id of the family.

"I'd rather do it now and get paid for it, than have to do it after you guys die," he suggested in a rather too businesslike tone of voice.

"Fair enough."

Our unfinished basement is scary. Half of it is too low to stand up in, causing Brian to navigate around it like a troll with scoliosis. There is a damp patch on one wall that I keep spritzing with anti-mould poisons, and the drain in the floor suffers reflux after heavy rains. There was our Barbie-sized set of washer and dryer; we had tried several times to install new machines, but the turn down into the basement was too narrow; we'd have to tear down the walls to get new appliances down there. So eventually, we gave up and began using the local laundromat. We did this for three years until we finally caved in and repaired the original dwarf appliances.

Sometimes late at night I would lie in bed and think about the basement and all the things that were down there:

Two mirrored doors. A slab of cedar from a 40-year-old home-made bed frame. Suitcases full of orphaned electronic cables. My old Selectric typewriter and Brian's first manual, an Underwood. The red Afghan tribal dress my girlfriends gave me for my birthday in 1972, which I still hope to fit into again. Five drums. Two roasting pans. Snarls of Christmas lights. Dale Carnegie books on how to influence people, from my parents' shelves. A crate of cookbooks I have never used. And many banker boxes fill with drafts of plays, books, and screenplays, the things I'd written that had come to light, or not. Typing typing typing.

Cartons full of Casey's high-school books, university essays, sketches, journals; metal filing cabinets full of Brian's interviews with Madonna and Mick Jagger and Michael J. Fox. Stars in the cellar.

The bothersome part was that none of this—the letters, the drill bits, the bolts of Chinese silk, and lumpy pillows—was accounted for. It represented both the worthless things we hadn't bothered to throw out along with the treasures that we have not treasured. In Burlington, the basement was where the family imagination held sway, where my mother painted or fired pottery. Our basement, for all its evidence of diligence, had become the graveyard of our care-lessness.

Every now and then I would try to take a stab at it, carting garbage bags of clothing to the Goodwill, throwing out the talk-show mugs and the posters for long-forgotten events. But this is not a one-person job, and Brian is less haunted by the basement than I am. To put it in a positive light, he is better at archiving. In his line of work, he is also the recipient of a steady stream of film-industry swag that walks the line between hopeless junk and stuff I can't bring myself to throw out. His passions come with many material objects attached to them, too: conga drums, a 30-pound bag of percussion instruments, camera tripods, computer drives. Gear. Stuff.

On the other hand, the obsessively rewritten lost novels and the rolling racks of clothing in the basement are mostly mine. The other day I pulled out a 1980s pair of knee-high suede boots whose time had come round again. If only novels were like boots.

If Brian catches me making a pile of stuff to throw out, he will go through it and reclaim things.

"Why are you keeping your press pass from the Cannes Film Festival of eight years ago?" I will ask.

"I collect my press passes."

For the last two years, Casey had been eyeing the items he had inherited from us. The useful things (the silver family flask, his grandfather's three-piece suit, my old Pentax), the pointless things (a microwave omelette maker), and the junk (thousands of paper drink umbrellas).

Now it was time to get rid of it.

■

Down in the basement, we began sorting. He held up a strange garden implement, a long metal pole with a spidery set of prongs on one end.

"What is this?"

"It's for twisting out weeds," I said defensively. "It's so I don't have to bend over." Casey does not have to point out how unweeded the garden remains.

"This is the kind of stuff we have a million of," he said.

He finds my chromatic harmonica, which I never use, and plays a tune on it.

"How's it going with this?"

I take it away and put it on the "keep" pile. I plan to play the harmonica when I am old and bedridden. Casey rummages on.

"Dad would never do this, you know."

"He doesn't have the time."

"Anyway he'd just want to pay someone to do it, and nobody but me could sort all this out, what's valuable, what's not."

"That's true. But if we'd been more organized, we would have thrown out our old vinyl."

"What about this?" He held up a chipped china baby's plate.

"That's my great-grandmother's baby plate; that stays," I said. I pulled out an oil painting my mother had done, yet another still life with flowers. Maybe reframed? I didn't have the heart to throw it out. This was, I realized, how people ended up on reality TV shows about compulsive hoarding.

We began to paw through a dreadful dark space under the stairs, the Swag Hole, where we tossed the cheap bags and satchels that Brian brings home from the film festival circuit.

"There must be over 20 in here," said Casey, pulling out a tangle of logo-festooned items. "Talk about baggage."

We looked into the maw, where one last suitcase lurked. An old-fashioned hard-shell one. I clicked it open to find a nest of mould and my first bits of published work. Yellow carbon copies of book reviews I had written in my twenties, when carbon copies still existed. Letters from my high-school boyfriend. Some were too damp to salvage, but most were fine. I sat down in a broken chair and began reading one.

"See, if you just keep plowing through it, valuable things turn up," said Casey the archivist.

"We have to stop doing this," I finally said, "or we'll get sick. The mould is bad." It was hard to make him stop, though. He was on a dumpster bender.

Then we began The Removal, hauling up lumber, cobwebby baseboards, defunct sewing machines, and roof racks. The front yard filled up. Soon there was a small ski hill of matter.

"Take a picture," Casey said. "We need to document this." I stood on the sidewalk to get a long shot of the heap with Casey posing on top, like a climber summiting.

"Sure you don't want this lovely batik from Bali?" I said, waving a wall hanging at him. He looked at me to make sure I was kidding.

"And I guess you don't want a sink shaped like a seashell," I said, admiring the dainty model we had ripped out of the bathroom when we moved in. He got into the cab of the truck.

"It's time to hit the dump."

On the way down Parliament Street in the truck, we rolled open the windows. The breeze felt good, drying the sweat we had worked up. The truck engine was gratifyingly loud, a workhorse of an engine. We stopped at the lights, glanced sideways, and met the eyes of a row of people.

"Hey, we're on the same level as the streetcar," Casey said approvingly. I began to see the appeal of driving your own U-Haul.

The city dump is down by the lake, in an unkempt industrial area on Commissioners Street. I've always had a secret affection for the street, an under-travelled straightaway in an area of scrap metal yards and cavernous film studios, alternating with fields of wildflowers and weeds. I used to come down here with a college flame in his father's car. He'd drive right out into the middle of one of these fields of Queen Anne's lace and ragweed, tilt the front seat back as far as it would go, and we'd make out with Toronto's skyline sparkling ahead of us, like the screen of a drive-in movie. It was an ungroomed part of town, the place where freighters come to anchor and then rust for years. The place where things wind up.

We spotted a tall brick building with a concrete ramp leading up into it. It was ominous, that entrance, faintly evocative of gas chambers or something furtive and dire. In one corner of the parking lot, a man in a jumpsuit and a mask was sorting out Hazardous Wastes. He invited us to unload our paint cans. There was a pyramid of shrink-wrapped TVs near him, metal drums full of discarded paint, and a tower of dead car batteries.

The dozen half-empty cans of paint lurking at the back of our basement had been lightly but persistently on my mind ever since we'd moved in. Now we handed them over, and the young man in the gas mask poured some of the citrus colour from our living-room walls into a metal drum. It swirled in with the residue of other houses.

Casey lugged the Selectric out of the truck. I realized that I missed my old typewriter, the loud hum of it and the absolutely committed thwack of its keys. It throbbed like a beast and you really felt you were getting down to work when you typed on it. But away it went, to machine heaven.

"So where do we go for lumber and where for straight garbage?" Casey asked.

"Around the back for recycling, and straight up the ramp for things you're just throwing away. But you have to weigh in first. It's the next turn up the road."

At the weighing station, they gave us a "before" weight so that when we checked out they would know how much to charge us for the load. Ten bucks per 50 kilos of junk. This faintly thrilled me; in a very small way, we were becoming accountable.

An incongruously well-tended garden flanked the bottom of the ramp to the dump. With the engine gunning, we shot to the top.

"Why do we have to go up so high just to throw things away?" I asked. There was a sensation of motoring toward the end of a long dock, like the last scene in *Jules et Jim*, where the three of them drive off into the pier into the water.

"I don't know. Maybe it's about using gravity to get stuff into the incinerator." A long white tube angled down from the side of the dump to the place where things were burnt.

A man in a construction hat and a flare-orange vest took our receipt at the entrance. We inched into the dumpsite, a vast chamber with a great multicoloured cliff of garbage bulldozed against one corner and a fresh, uncompressed boreal forest of debris in the other.

"Just back up to the active pile and unload," the worker told us. Wow, I thought, I didn't realize we could play such a personal role in the disposal process. There were no intermediaries or agreeable facades here, just a cascade of discarded crap, onto which you hurled your stuff. The pile was the opposite of possessions, with which we insulate ourselves from unpleasant realities, like rot and death. We go to so much trouble, installing lengths of quarter round to cover up the unseemly seam in our houses, where the floors meet the walls. But in the end, it all goes on the slag heap. There was something exhilarating in being at the bedside, as it were, of all the objects we were ready to leave behind.

A brown station wagon full of old fencing pulled up beside us, and a middle-aged man got out with a springy step to pop the trunk. He glanced our way.

"We have to stop meeting like this," I said as a joke. Luckily, he laughed.

"Yeah, but who would guess, eh?"

Casey and I got into the back of the U-Haul and began hurling objects onto the loose scree of garbage. Old mops, a bristleless broom, bent curtain rods, the worn Turkish rug I had bought for our first apartment.

I threw the curtain rods in a high arc, like javelins. They pierced a gutted mattress. Casey tossed a box full of mouldy paperbacks onto the pile.

"This is fun, isn't it?" I said, putting my arm into it.

We were making more noise than was strictly necessary. The man in the station wagon began to chuck his lumber, and a rhythm sprang up between the three of us. After all the hemming and hawing, the careful evaluation of what should stay or go, this fiesta of letting go felt good.

I turned to admire the more processed slope of debris in the other corner, impressionist in its flecks of colour. The pile was intricate and beautiful; it had broken down the identity of the individual objects but not their detail, their thingness. The rampart had a human presence.

When the truck was empty of everything except wood, we drove down the sloping exit and past the boat-sized recycling containers. We visited the graveyard of spavined appliances and old slack-jawed refrigerators. There was a pile of white ash inside a garage that rose to a delicate tip, like a heap of salt. The residue from the incinerator, probably. Ramp, dump, tunnel, flames—so many stages before the garbage disappeared, and even then it fanned out into the air, not yet invisible.

The stubbornness of our stuff.

We drove through the weighing station where we were asked to pay $31. I was euphoric and had to restrain myself from tipping.

It was almost six o'clock, with that late-August slant of light that means fall and getting down to business. We rolled open the windows; the air felt cooler here down by the lake. Brian was at the office, finishing up a story. I phoned to tell him the good news about our defoliated basement and how much work we'd done. Luckily he didn't ask whether we'd thrown out his goat-claw percussion shakers. After 30 years of living together and 26 years of parenthood, our roles had become well defined; it was his job to hang onto things (including me), my job to feel oppressed by the basement, and it fell to Casey to tell us what was worth keeping and what we should discard.

We ate at the pub on Parliament, raising a glass of beer to our labours. We'd worked well together, perhaps because he was in the driver's seat this time. And when I had taken my mother's painting back inside the house, he hadn't argued.

I set off to visit my mother in Burlington. Every time I saw her now she came swimming back from a more distant shore, but she was still hanging in there. I found new pleasure in these last visits, so shorn of everything unnecessary from the past. Just the two of us, talking and not always making sense.

Casey went to drop the truck off. Then he and some friends were going to down to the spit, a long peninsula of land that juts out into the lake. It was still warm enough for bonfires on the beach. Brian was up in the goth-castle of the Rogers building, waiting for his story to be edited and put to bed. The city was more than big enough for all of us.

The Future

ALTHOUGH I KNEW I could always count on my parents to bail me out financially, I never had to ask them; a benign economy shone down on the young, and life was easy—perhaps easier than it ever will be again. In 1971, I could get by (and travel for months at a time) on the money I earned writing a free-lance book-review column for a newspaper. Quaint skills! Roughly the equivalent of working as a blacksmith today. Or ... being a nar-whal impersonator. I can't think of anything that's arcane enough to convey just how obsolete my first job has become.

Astutely, my parents saw writing as an insecure pursuit. But what did they know? Our parents didn't share our music or our values. Many of us mistrusted the very concept of family, a bour-geois institution (we said) created to oppress women and shore up the patriarchy. "They fuck you up, your mum and dad" begins the famous poem from that year, by Philip Larkin.

Hmmm. There's still some truth in this, but nobody seems to have come up with a better arrangement than "family," regardless of the genders or sexual persuasions involved, for raising children, tol-erating our fellow human beings, and helping each other through life. Family is a jalopy, not a Porsche, but it takes us down the road.

I saw an article in the real estate section of the paper the other day about a mother who was building an adorable little cabin, 10 by 12 feet square, on the property behind her house, where her 24-year-old college-student daughter could live rent-free. In Italy, this is nothing new; a study published by the London Centre for Economics reported that a mind-boggling 85 percent of Italian men aged 18 to 34 still live with their parents. Even when the daughters are factored in, the percentage of grown kids living with their parents in Italy is still over 50 per cent. According to a recent *Guardian* article, one minister has called for a new law forcing "*bamboccioni*" (mummies' boys and girls) to leave home at 18. And when they leave, the maternal ties often remain. One bachelor in Rome ships his laundry to his mother in Bari on Friday and gets his shirts back ironed perfectly by Monday.

Does this protracted family life undermine our kids' independence, or are we just helping them tackle a much tougher world than the one we grew up in?

Now that my son and I have met on the other side of the leaving-home dramas, I've come to the conclusion that these lingering familial bonds might be a good thing: signs of a return to normal clannishness after an era of hard-core individualism. The deal used to be that kids left home at 18 to "find themselves." Then the day they turned 21 they magically became adults. Many of our parents did just that, putting on shirts and ties, getting married, having babies at an age when today's kids are still binge-drinking or applying to business schools.

But what if this pattern—leaving home at the end of adolescence—is the real historical aberration, and the current tendency of sticking closer to home for longer periods marks a return to normal? This is what crossed Casey's mind when he first travelled in Mexico, where everyone he met asked, "Where is your family?"

"Delayed transition" is the sociological term for this new tendency in families. In previous centuries, children rarely left the shade of the family tree; sons grew up to work alongside their fathers in the family business or girls married the boy from two farms over. Then the industrial revolution arrived, driving workers into urban areas, and the era of modern travel began. Children who left home had to go farther afield, *sans* cellphone. Corporations transferred employees and scattered families all over the globe, in the hard-to-fathom days before the communications revolution.

But email and Skype have made geographical separation almost a non-issue. Everyone is more often in touch with everyone, including parents and their kids.

If we think of grown children staying close to the family (not necessarily under the same roof, but looped in) as *normal* rather than a sign of arrested adolescence, then where did we get the idea that kids should leave home at 18?

I think it may have arisen from circumstances that have nothing to do with the natural curve of childhood development: the spread of post-secondary education from the rich to the middle class; and the outbreak of two world wars. At 18, children (mostly boys) either left home to go off to college or to fight in wars. And because these teenagers undertook the responsibilities of fighting in a war, we assumed they came back home as grown men.

But ask any mother who has lost a son in combat: a 19-year-old is a boy. War may prematurely age (or kill) its young soldiers but it doesn't necessarily turn them into adults. Leaving home and growing up are separate enterprises.

■

Part of the problem when I try to imagine the future is this: I can't. The future used to be so easy to visualize, a Jetsons landscape of housecleaning robots and mono-cars that glide along on elevated rails. Life in this cartoon world-to-come where everyone wears jumpsuits is zippy and homogeneous. Now it feels as if the very concept of The Future belongs to the past. Whenever I try to envision my son embedded in some future landscape, there's a mist around it (or a pall). The details won't come into focus. It's not that I lack faith in him—it's the things I can't imagine that lie ahead. Forty years ago, political issues were more circumscribed, wars had clear boundaries, and Canada was the ho-hum country where nothing bad could happen. Now pandemics, environmental dramas, and terrorism are a potential threat to even the most sheltered child.

With good reason, parents see the future as an edgy, competitive, unforgiving place, and we want our kids to have what it takes to cope with it. But you never know which qualities will equip your child for the world, in ways his parents can't understand. The DIY kid might be more nimble than the deep and narrow PhD. We need to have faith in our kids' sometimes wacky instincts about how to navigate the future.

I am surprised to find that more and more I do have faith. Even though I'm anxious about the obstacles still ahead of him, I feel optimistic at heart. I am beginning to believe that his resistance to the more traditional routes is part of an ongoing canny, intuitive adaptation to a new world. (Perhaps it qualifies as "evolution.") "It's like I'm doing my own unofficial graduate program," he says about his industrious, self-regulated days of multiple jobs, ambitious creative endeavours, and social networking. He's paying his rent, and hanging onto his dreams, as he acquires the skills, knowledge, and values that will take him forward, *in ways I cannot imagine.*

Just when our kids need forbearance, support, and maybe some benign neglect around the topic of careers, they're more likely to encounter our fear that they will "lose their place" if they take too long figuring things out. But they don't need more nervousness; my son looks over his shoulder too.

The world *is* precarious. We want to see our kids on a foolproof, well-lit path. But that safe path no longer exists. It's a wraparound frontier now.

■

It was a family gathering a few days after the death of my mother, at the age of 99. Brian had put together a slide show with some old photographs of my mother's life, from a startled, round-faced baby in 1911 to a college student in a black wool bathing suit doing head-stands on a beach. Then a bride in a tailored suit and hat with one foot on the runner of a Model T Ford; a new mother in front of her house, slightly frowning; finally, a grandmother in a fuchsia shirt laughing and brandishing her sherry glass. I told the people gath-ered in my parents' former living room a few stories about her. Then the grandsons spoke up.

"She was always doing something, or making something, and I would do it with her," said Daniel, who has become a gifted visual artist. "Whether it was painting, or cooking, or raking the garden. I learned alongside her."

My nephew Jake was partly raised by my parents for his first eight years, after his parents split up. Full of emotion, Jake simply said thank you to his grandmother for everything she'd done. Then Casey, the middle grandson, got up to say a few words.

Our family tends not to dress up for special occasions, but he had ironed his good white shirt and put on his suit. He wore leather shoes, polished, and his hair was combed back, just like my father in his youth. It was a nod to the importance of family rituals and a tribute to my dapper dad.

Standing in the middle of a room filled with friends and neigh-bours, he said that when he was little he took his grandparents and their benevolent, broadloomed realm for granted. He came for visits, ate the dinner especially prepared with his allergies and appetites in mind, then escaped the dinner table to eat his second

211

dessert while watching cartoons in the den. He assumed that this cared-for world was just one corner of a bigger, similarly forgiving universe.

"It took a while before I realized that they had created this world for us and that it didn't just exist on its own."

There were a few nods around the room. I wondered if we were going to be able to give our grandchildren the same sense of a warm, coherent environment (with less beige broadloom) in which to thrive. That was what we ran away from. But our children who won't leave home or the ones who come back are more grown up, in many ways, than us.

Epilogue

I AM AT HOME, in my office, surrounded by piles of book manuscript on the floor. The yellow Post-its that curl up from many of the pages represent edits still to be done. The deadline is close. Cunningly, I have shifted the focus of my anxiety from my grown son to this pile of paper. But my main worry is the title. I've come up with 26 of them, but none that pass muster with my publisher, my family, and me.

If you try to think about titles for too long, you eventually lose all perspective. You start choosing random lines from songs by Beck, and they all sound brilliant.

This has already happened to me by 2 p.m. when Brian comes into the room.

"Any luck?" he asks.

"How about *I Really Must Be Going Now*."

A tactful pause. "I think it's a bit arch."

"But it's funny. Isn't it? They're keen on funny."

"But the book's not that funny," he points out.

"I know. It's semi-tragic. People keep dying in it. I warned them not to expect Erma Bombeck."

I turn around and notice for the first time that his mouth looks strange, kind of rubbery, and that he's pale. Then I remember; he has just had a root canal.

"Oh, your mouth, right! How was it?"

He shrugs, and his lips ripple experimentally before he speaks.

"It was okay. And when they were giving me the nitrous oxide, I was sure I had come up with the perfect title for you."

"Really? On nitrous? What?" I was getting desperate. Maybe drugs really were the answer.

His lips form a sort of square.

"*Consent.*"

We laugh, which causes his mouth to do odd things.

"Well, it's a great title for book about date rape," I say.

"What's wrong with the one from last night—*How We Leave Home*? Doesn't anybody like that?"

"Not really. Barbara said it might end up in the 'How To' section of the bookstore. And Janet thought I said 'Howie Leaves Home.' She thought it was a children's book about a duck."

"Last night when I was walking by the lake, I came up with an idea for the subtitle. *The Far Shore of Motherhood.*"

"Hmmm. Nice."

"Because there *is* a lake theme in the book . . ."

". . . which only you will notice . . ."

Brian massages his jaw.

"What about *Sugar Mountain*?" I say. "The Neil Young song? It's actually a song about being 20 and leaving home."

His brow furrows.

"I'm not sure mothers of small children would want to buy a book called *Sugar Mountain* . . . ," he tentatively offers.

"With the subtitle *Feel The Rush!* Okay, I see your point, forget it. Although, kids might buy it. They'd buy that and *Howie Leaves Home* for sure."

It's after 2 p.m., and I'm still in my nightgown. I push some of the manuscript piles around with my bare feet, fanning them out.

"*I Really Must Be Going* is still my favourite. It's what someone says when they know they should be leaving, and then don't. It's the malingering mother, always threatening to go, but still sitting there with her coat on."

He peers at the long file of potential titles open on my screen. His white hair at the back of his head is all ruffled up from being in the dentist's chair.

"Are you sure you shouldn't lie down for a while?" I say.

"No, I've got too much stuff to do."

"Well, don't worry about me. I've got two more days. No need to panic."

Brian is someone who does the Sunday *New York Times* crossword until every box is filled. I see him mentally rolling up his sleeves.

"What about *Mothering Up*—that's upbeat. Or—wait—*Mothering Down* . . . or . . . *Too Close to Home* . . . or—"

I swivel in my ergonomic chair and put my arms around him. It's a strange assignment I have chosen, to come up with a working title for our lives, but I'm glad he's still game.

Acknowledgements

The inklings of this project began with a preface I wrote for *Double* 217 *Lives*, a literary anthology about motherhood and the writing life. I'd like to thank Shannon Cowan, Fiona Lam and Cathy Stonehouse for inviting me to contribute. The piece I wrote for them became a scene in this book and got me thinking about our relationship as parents to our grown-up children.

However, it was my editor, Patrick Crean, who came to me with the idea, and I am grateful for his faith in the project. I'm sure we both thought it would be a simple undertaking. But becoming an embedded reporter in one's own family has its disorienting moments. I counted on Patrick's support, good judgement and encouragement at every step along the way.

The chapter "That's That" has been adapted from the story "Just Cremation," which appeared in the anthology *The Heart Does Break*, published by Random House. Part of the chapter entitled "The Broken Year" first appeared in an essay for *Zoomer* magazine. My sincere thanks to editors Jean Baird and Kim Izzo for their guidance.

I did my best to be home-free while I worked on this book, by moving from nest to nest. I am grateful to Katherine Ashenberg,

Anne Nicholson and Arne Moore, John Barrington and Tina Vanderheyden, and the Queen St. Dark Horse café for providing writing refuges.

The chapter "Vertical Travel" is based on conversations with my godson, Gabriel Czarnecki, who generously shared his knowledge and ideas about rite of passage ceremonies. Mark Czarnecki helped me sort out the sixties. Thanks to Christy Mackintosh for her Tunnel Mountain research.

My friend and colleague Nora Underwood turned the copyediting process into a pleasurable dialogue, and I am grateful for her deft editorial insights as well. My appreciation to Wendy Thomas at Thomas Allen Publishers for grace under pressure, and to my agent, Samantha Haywood, for her early endorsement. To Jill Frayne for always checking in. For manuscript reads I'm indebted to Ian Pearson, Brian Johnson, Casey Johnson, Christopher Keil and Barbara Gowdy. From the first outline-on-a-napkin to the final draft, Mike Kearns provided counsel. Many thanks to my comrades who escorted me through the title ordeal, in particular to Anne Mackenzie. Janet Burke provided perspective and ER support, as always.

At this point, authors normally acknowledge their loved ones, without whom the book would not be possible, etc. In my case, this has never been truer. Let me thank my beloved narrative elements, Brian and Casey, from the bottom of my heart. I am lucky to have two big-spirited men in my life, and I owe everything to their creativity, honesty and generosity.